Contents

PART THREE

**Recognize, Revise, and Internalize:
Changing the RA Way of Life   145**

Acknowledgments

I wrote this book not only as a follow-up to *Girl Wars*, but because of female friends and colleagues who have been un–relationally aggressive and supportive over the years. It seems important to look at what goes right in relationships as well as what can go wrong. To Susan, Beth, Maureen, Shelba, Pat, Stacy, Sherry, Adria, Kathleen, Monica, Robin, Lisa, Gail, Barb, and many, many more: thank you! And to Teryn Johnson, a patient and positive editor who weathered the storms of this book with me, much gratitude.

Introduction

When I was eight, my mother gathered with other women to sit in the courtyard of our apartment complex. All summer, after her housework was completed, she would be there, in the center of a cluster of aluminum chairs, gathered with friends to drink ice tea and smoke cigarettes while all the children played nearby. There is a black-and-white picture of the group somewhere—they have haircuts and clothes that have gone out of style and come back in, and they are smiling and happy, just as I remember them.

As our family moved on and lived in other places, a constant of my childhood was my mother's friends and female acquaintances. There was always a diverse crowd of women in her life, ready to help celebrate holidays, mourn tragedies, or just talk about the events of an ordinary day. I can't recall my mother ever being mean to another woman, having a serious disagreement with one of her friends, or ending a relationship due to a dispute. She has had friends for decades: Bev, Evelyn, Gertrude, Joyce, Jane, Ingrid, Irene—the list is long. When my dad retired, these women made a quilt for my mom out of squares they each created; it was king-size and took a lot of effort.

It's no surprise that like my mother, I rely on and value my female friends, both the lifelong ones and those I know only through the Internet. I'm continually grateful for women who come into my life unexpectedly and give me the gift of themselves (like my neighbor Lisa Plotkin, who volunteered to read and critique this entire manuscript while she nursed her newborn son).

Then there are women I dread to be near, who sometimes

seem as plentiful as the women I cherish. They are the ones who are stuck in that middle school "bee" behavior: the Queen Bee bullies (a particularly memorable one buzzed furiously around me on my first job, as if she actually was protecting "her" hive from intruders); the Middle Bees, who spread gossip or stand by as others do so; and Afraid-to-Bee victims, who retreat into passivity. Encounters with any of these women are painful reminders of the teen years, when female bullying is at its peak and mean girls don't hesitate to use words, gestures, or behaviors to wound another. Women who get stuck in these roles are still involved in the same harmful dynamic years later: Queen Bees bully their way to the top, Middle Bees serve as the go-betweens, and Afraid-to-Bee victims are targeted for aggression. It isn't confined to the work setting, either. These situations play out in virtually any place where women gather—even online.

Like many women, I have found myself playing each of the "bee" roles. There have been times when I responded to a threat with aggression, got caught up in a gossip fest that was downright malicious, or withdrew from another woman in frightened silence. Until I wrote a book for adolescent girls, I didn't realize there was a name for those behaviors: relational aggression (RA or female bullying).

During interviews and talks about that book, I was asked again and again if RA stops after high school. Many of the men and women who posed that question already had their own answers, as did I. When I searched through existing literature for confirmation, I found no in-depth discussion of RA in adult women. There were books on nasty bosses and some on hostile women, but I had a sense that the scope and magnitude of RA extended well beyond the workplace and often involved more than one bully and one victim.

Are there midlife mean bees? Do grown women gossip and campaign against other women in an attempt to bring them down? Are there cliques in the corporate lunchroom as well as the car pool? Can older women be as two-faced and competitive as their younger counterparts? As I talked to women—the true experts on these behaviors—their resounding response was, yes!

Consider what these women have to say:

Yes, other women definitely look down on me because I'm a stay-at-home mom and didn't even leave a successful career to take care of my family. When we go to a party or someplace where there are adults of both genders, men are more likely to accept me as a stay-at-home mom than other women.

Tanya, age thirty-two, mother of two young children

I swam competitively in high school, but it was cake compared to my experience with the group of women I worked out with not too long ago. Guys don't like it when I'm faster than them, but these women were worse, acting offended to share a lane with me and making rude comments about my body or the length of my workouts. At this point, I swim for fun, not to compete, so I dropped out and decided I'm better off exercising alone.

Barb, age twenty-nine

It's like playing a game of cards, only your kids help you win. Everyone is out to "trump" everyone else with some new accomplishment of her son or daughter.

Tessa, age twenty-six, part of a mother's organization

The jealousy among the women here is unbelievable. They watch each new person who moves in to see if he or she might own something valuable, and the gossip is incredible. The men do their own thing, but the women notice and comment on everything!

Sasha, age seventy, who lives in a retirement center

The pages that follow contain stories from women around the world who encountered mean girls grown up and have something to say about it. I obtained these stories in a variety of ways: through ads for submissions in writing magazines, women's publications, and Web sites; fliers sent to conferences; and word-of-mouth. This book contains a sampling of the best pieces I received. Some of the women who wrote were Queen Bee bullies and others were Afraid-to-Bee victims who had suffered through months, years, or a lifetime of abuse. Middle Bee women, those who had found themselves in between the aggressor and her target in one way or another, also shared their experiences.

Other parts of the book contain material from women who were interviewed to obtain input on how aggression plays out in specific groups, such as the very young or old and those from ethnically diverse backgrounds. Experts who have helped women overcome the impact of aggression in one way or another contributed as well.

Where details of a story would be damaging to an individual who could be identified, the story was edited to preserve the content but protect confidentiality. Contributors had the choice of using their real name or a pen name. If you want to contact any of the contributors or experts, e-mail me at opheliasmother@aol.com.

Rather than share a litany of abuses and lead readers to believe women really are just mean and nasty, the focus of this book is on changing behavior and developing relationships with other women that help rather than harm. At any age, Queen Bees, Middle Bees, or Afraid-to-Bees can transform their behavior by shifting away from an aggressive dynamic and embracing a spirit of cooperation and collegiality in interactions with others. Victims, bullies, or in-betweeners caught in the trap of RA at home, work, or play *do* have alternatives. Many of the contributors offer their opinions on this topic, and the third part of the book describes specific steps that can be taken to deal with aggression or passivity.

You may feel you will never be able to escape mean girls. Don't despair. Although female relationships full of rivalry, jealousy, or maliciousness may be poisoning your life right now, change is always possible. Even if bee-type behaviors have plagued you since adolescence, you can now take advantage of new opportunities for positive connections with other women. This book first helps you identify *what* adult RA is, then describes *how* it affects women like yourself in a variety of situations, and finally, *shows* what can be done about it.

PART ONE

Relational Aggression 201

The Who, What, and Why of RA

You've always been there, even in
Kindergarten, pushing my face into
a can of worms on the playground.
In grade school, calling me a witch
and telling me you'll burn me
at the stake at recess.
In middle school, you didn't want to
be my friend, you said I was weird,
too smart, too serious.
High school moments of pure hell,
of National Honor Society,
leads in school plays. Kisses of death.
In college, I kept to myself,
stayed clear of your jealousy,
alone with my own self-loathing.
In the real world, at every job,
you've always gone out of your way
to hurt me.

ALIZA SHERMAN, "TAKE ME DOWN"

CHAPTER 1

All Grown Up and Ready to Sting

Adult Female Aggression

Mean girls grow up to be mean women,
make no mistake about that.

—A WOMAN CALLER TO A RADIO TALK SHOW ON BULLYING

I t happens when you least expect it: the sudden, painful sting that hurts deeply, because you thought you were in a safe place, with other women and immune from harm. A word, a gesture, or some other seemingly innocuous behavior can be all it takes to wound in a way that hurts more than any physical blow. This is female relational aggression (RA): the subtle art of emotional devastation that takes place every day at home, at work, or in community settings. Unlike openly aggressive men, women learn early on to go undercover with these assaults, often catching their victims unaware. Many carry this behavior into adulthood.

What Is Relational Aggression?

RA is the use of relationships to hurt another, a way of verbal violence in which words rather than fists inflict damage. RA seems to peak in the early teen years when girls use a variety of behaviors that wound without ever pulling a punch. Word wars are often dismissed as "just the way girls are," or "she's just jealous." Whether or not you're a mother, you probably understand these scenarios intuitively: the girl who gets excluded from a crowd she previously belonged to; the newcomer who fails to be accepted by other girls no matter what she does; the girl who is somehow different and targeted for that reason; or the popular Queen Bee, who buzzes from place to place spreading discomfort and manipulating others with her words. Sounds pretty juvenile, doesn't it?

Unfortunately, some women never outgrow these behaviors, turning into adults who slay with a smile and wound with a word. The mean girls of middle school may change into grown-up "shrews," "witches," "prima donnas," and "bitches," but underneath, the same game that started in grade school is still being played. In and out of the workplace, as individuals and in groups, these women continue to interact in aggressive ways reminiscent of high school hallways where girls jockeyed for social status.

After encounters with such women, you walk away wondering exactly what happened, and, sometimes, why you care so much. In a search for answers, you may even reflect back on your adolescent years, when behaviors such as jealousy, gossip, and forming cliques were the modus operandi. You may remember the moments when you sighed thankfully, thinking it was all behind you. The end result, when you discover it isn't, is feelings of confusion, hurt, and even fear. Consider the following real-life situations:

Rhonda, age thirty-four, is one of twenty-five female secretaries at a midsize legal firm. Her boss, impressed by Rhonda's computer skills, suggests she go for further training so she can help with the information technology needs of the firm. He offers to accommodate her time away for classes if she will agree to stay with the firm for a year after she finishes. When Rhonda tells her coworkers about the opportunity, they congratulate her, but in the weeks that follow, the emotional climate of the office grows noticeably cooler. Within a month of starting classes, Rhonda is no longer invited to lunch with the other women, and they frequently "forget" to pass on important messages that arrive while she is in class.

"What did I do wrong?" Rhonda asks Marci, the only coworker who isn't shunning her.

"Can't you see it?" Marci answers. "They're all jealous because you're getting an opportunity they aren't."

• • •

Tina, an attractive twenty-two-year old, is one of three women participating in a corporate internship that will result in a job offer for one of them. So far, she is the strongest candidate for the position, which will involve working directly with the company's male CEO. One morning during a coffee break, Alice, one of the other interns, comes into the break room where Tina and the CEO are deep in conversation about a work project.

"Oh—*excuse me!*" Alice says loudly, a knowing smile on her face. Both Tina and the CEO invite her to stay, but she hurries out without another word.

A few days later, Tina finds herself alone in an elevator with Beth, the third intern.

"So, I hear things are really heating up between you and the CEO," Beth comments.

Blushing, Tina stammers, "What are you talking about?"

"Oh come on, Tina, you know exactly what I'm talking about. Everyone in the office does. You're sleeping with him just so you can get the job."

Sharon, the forty-year-old mother of teenaged Susanna, decides to volunteer for the band parents group at her daughter's high school. When Sharon takes her lunch hour early so she can attend the first meeting, the six other moms already there are slow to acknowledge her. When the meeting runs late, Sharon apologetically gathers up her things and puts on her coat.

"I'm sorry. I have to get back to work," she explains.

"Oh, you're a *working mom*," one of the women comments, exchanging a knowing glance with the others.

Same Behavior, Different Age

The incidents just described involving adult women are not so different from the teenager shunned by her friends, talked about in the hallways, or excluded from activities by other girls. Mean behavior exists on a continuum for both adolescents and adults. In an attempt to understand why, Judith Sutphen, a former director for the Vermont Commission on Women, met with a group of 130 teenage girls to discuss self-esteem and interactions with others. In the following excerpt from her report, Sutphen offers a possible explanation for why women may act to undermine one another and the consequences that result:

There's been a lot of attention focused lately on mean girls. . . . "Relational aggression" is the new buzzword for girls who tease, insult, threaten, maliciously gossip, play cruel games with their best friends' feelings and establish exclusive cliques and hierarchies in high school. Writers try to reassure us that it's not that girls are born mean; they just get that way when they're with other girls.

. . . All the attention has made me think about why girls learn to hurt through relationships, and how this translates into our lives as grown women.

Perhaps girls don't necessarily want to be mean, they just want to be. "Be" in the sense of personal power, the kind that everybody wants. The shortest path to this goal for a girl, the Morrisville teens told us, is to be with a guy.

It's not until a lot later that they realize that maybe this power-through-another is not exactly what they were looking for.

But it's what they know.

Bringing all this into grown-up life as women, we are often ill prepared to support one another as some gain access to public power on their own. Women supervisors frequently note that directing male employees is easier than directing female employees. Women who are bold enough to step into public life through politics or the media are often most harshly critiqued by their own gender and held to a double standard in their accomplishments. Perhaps we've learned those girlhood games too well.

It's time to unlearn them.

In her book *Meeting at the Crossroads: Women's Psychology and Girl's Development*, Dr. Carol Gilligan adds further insight to this issue. She stresses that while both girls and boys desire genuine connections with others, girls mature through forging relationships rather than separating from them, which makes the failure to connect so problematic.

When there is a persistent failure to bond, to be heard, and to be understood, girls learn unhealthy relational patterns that can last into adulthood. The results can be long lasting: The head of a clique of mean girls in middle school aggressively makes her way through high school and college and bullies her way to the top in career or volunteer pursuits. The go-between girl who learns to survive by staying in the middle position continues to operate "behind the scenes" in adulthood. Tragically, the teen who believes she deserves the role of victim continues to place herself in a passive role in relationships long after she leaves the halls of high school.

Women who have never had true female friends, who avoid activities because they involve women, who disparage women as a group, or who deliberately work in male-dominated environments because they don't like women are everyday examples of a basic failure to connect with peers. This theory could explain why RA is so much more common (but not exclusive) to females across the lifespan.

The Mature Bee

Relational aggression in younger women generally involves three players: the bully or aggressor, the victim or target, and the bystander, a girl in between who watches aggression occur but may or may not intervene. In adult women, it seems apparent that RA becomes much more deliberate as well as subtle, and the in-betweener may play a different role because adult women are less likely to stand by passively and watch such situations unfold. Some of these women even adopt a malicious variation of the in-between role. If a bully is the Queen Bee, her sidekick is often the Middle Bee, who isn't directly aggressive, but who creates a context where women with a tendency to respond aggressively to threats will do so. For example, the Middle Bee may be the woman who makes sure the Queen Bee bully hears all the office coffee break talk—twisted so that it reflects badly on her. The Middle

Bee woman senses which behaviors are guaranteed to incite a potential aggressor and doesn't hesitate to use them.

In the same way, the Afraid-to-Bee adult woman demonstrates the victim role perfectly. Unlike an adolescent girl whose forming identity is vulnerable to the slings and arrows of a bully, the Afraid-to-Bee is more aware of her abilities and often knows that her tormenting Queen Bee is unreasonable but lacks the confidence to respond assertively. She is truly afraid to be her own person.

Why Are Women Often Their Own Worst Enemies?

Many of the women who voiced opinions on this question said that power is the underlying motivation for adult RA—the power to manipulate members of the PTA, the power to control a corporate climate, or the power to dominate physically at the gym. Because women traditionally have little power, this line of thought suggests that the instant there is a perceived threat, aggression occurs as a protective mechanism.

Others believe women and men are naturally opposite in terms of roles and values. While women supposedly focus on nurturing and helpful relationships, men strive for power. Women want to make connections and be liked, while men want to achieve goals and be superior, even if that means alienating others.

Some suggest that low self-esteem propels a woman into an aggressive or passive stance, and that giving or accepting emotional abuse is all about the view one has of oneself. Regardless of her role as Queen Bee (constantly on the offense), Afraid-to-Bee (scared victim), or Middle Bee (always in between), according to this theory, hurtful female behavior is motivated by feelings of inferiority.

Then there's the suggestion that aggression is learned behavior. According to proponents of this belief, women who grew up in aggressive and violent situations or who learned to interact with others in particular ways as children are more likely to use those same behaviors to relate to others throughout life.

Evolutionary psychologists such as Dr. Anne Campbell (*Men, Women, and Aggression*) explain that women are not by nature violent. Aggression between women occurs as a genetic, protective drive to find the best circumstances to ensure the survival of children. Historically, this meant finding a protective male who was a good provider, but there are suggestions that this instinct to compete for resources may still motivate many women. That is, women are driven by a deeply ingrained biological need to acquire protection for their offspring, while men are motivated by acquisition and domination.

You might be the CEO of your own Fortune 500 company, according to these researchers, but underneath the power suit and between the networking lunches is a drive to care for and protect your "children," whether they are real, potential, or metaphorical (for example, clients, projects, employees, new business). In this world, women view other women as competitors for resources, with men being one of the more helpful resources. To that end, an evolutionist believes that all female interactions are part of a quest to ensure the survival of real or potential offspring.

Cognitive specialists stress another gender-based difference: men and women learn in different ways. Women attempt to see things from all perspectives and understand diverse points of view, while men frequently take an adversarial position and question new material.

A major cultural difference in men and women's roles is the emphasis placed on physical appearance. Women want to be attractive and men want to have attractive partners, which may result in rivalries within both genders.

All of these theories suggest that an undercurrent of competition may underlie female relationships, manifested in covert forms of aggression such as undermining, manipulation, and betrayal. Regardless of whether you buy the power theory, the self-esteem hypothesis, the learned behavior position, or the evolutionary psychology perspective (or some combination of all four) it is clear that RA is:

- Internally motivated
- Driven by a sense of threat or fear
- Used primarily by women
- A behavioral dynamic that can be changed with effort

Most experts agree that the aggressive Queen Bee is a victim in some ways, too, suffering from the same feelings of fear, anger, and lack of confidence she fosters in others. In fact, my work suggests that all women who get caught in the destructive dynamic of RA suffer in one way or another.

"Women who don't believe in themselves, who are threatened by others and see them as 'the enemy,' will lash out in an effort to make themselves feel more in control. In reality, they're not," explains Tia, a women's health counselor who has heard many stories of Queen Bee behavior. "But this isn't rational behavior we're talking about." She adds that victims and in-betweeners often experience the same conflicted emotions.

Undoing the Damage

The good news is that with help RA can be unlearned and more positive relationship skills adopted. Across the country, organizations geared to help girls have begun to show that there are ways to nurture a kinder, gentler breed of young woman who is able to use power in positive ways. Adult women are also learning to leave the "RA way" behind, as the following story demonstrates.

A Lifetime of Bullying Comes to an End
Lynne Matthews

At age twenty-four, I was passive, weak, and easily manipulated. I saw myself as a people pleaser, and I wanted everyone to like me. For most of my life, I had attracted friends who were the polar opposite; many were mean and demanding, and they bullied me.

When I was five, it was Linda, the girl across the street, who was my age. She made me do things I didn't want to do, like defy my mother, make fun of other girls, and lie. Bullying me was her greatest pleasure in life, and I was the prime victim. As a little girl, I was very responsible. If my mother told me to be home at a certain time, I was going to listen to her. One night, while Linda and I were playing handball against her garage as the sun went down, I had a feeling of dread, because I knew my mother was expecting me. When I told Linda I had to leave, she cornered me and said, "You aren't leaving. You're playing with me until I say."

"But—" I protested.

"No buts," she sneered, pointing to the ball. "Play!"

A little while later, I heard my mother calling my name from across the street, desperation in her voice. I was torn. Linda saw me hesitating and demanded that I keep playing even though my heart wasn't in it. Everything ended when my mother marched over to Linda's house, a scowl on her face. I couldn't please either one of them. I felt like a failure.

At age twenty-four, it was Marsha, another bully. She masked her bullying with her sense of humor by using a joking voice to get me to do what she wanted. I loved her wit and wanted to be around her all the time. She was funny and shocking, saying things to people I would never dream of uttering. Where I was shy and reserved, she was boisterous and loud. She would do anything to get her way and loved to make me do things for her. But if I didn't, watch out. She would barrage me with whiny threats like, "Come on, you have to do it or I'm going to be really pissed off," or "Don't be scared. You need to stand up for yourself!" If I still refused, she would get mean. "Come on, f——r," she would protest, using profanities to egg me on.

When Marsha moved into her own apartment about an hour away from me, it was a big deal. I would drive up there every so often and spend weekends with her. One evening, we decided to order Chinese food. The delivery boy arrived while Marsha was in the shower. I had just enough money to give him for the food and none left over for a tip. He totally understood. When Marsha found out, however, she was furious. "I can't believe you didn't give him a tip," she hissed. The next morning, she drove me to the takeout place and handed me a few dollars.

"Go," she said.

"What?" I asked. I had been under the impression we were going to the mall.

"Give him the tip. Say you were stupid and apologize. Those guys work hard. How would you feel?"

It was a horrible moment. My heart started to pound and I was angry, so deeply angry that I couldn't speak. "No," I finally said.

"Do it."

"No. I can't believe this."

"Do it. Come on, f——r," she said. "If you don't do this, you're a horrible person. He needs his tips. He works hard." She said it in her half-joking voice, but it was a threat: do it or you won't be my friend.

I got out of the car slowly, defeated. I went into the restaurant and explained who I was. I left the money in some girl's hand and got back into the car, slamming the door.

"See, was that so bad?" Marsha asked, already back in her teasing mode.

"No," I said, my head down.

Marsha and I are no longer friends. Last year, I decided that I was tired of being a doormat and questioned why I was attracting these types of friends. I explored it further. What was it about me that allowed this to happen? Why couldn't I stand up for myself? It was crazy. I seriously began to reevaluate my place in the world and realized that I needed to be strong. I thought back to that scared five-year-old. What did I expect to happen if I didn't do what Linda wanted? The bullying started with me, and it could end with me. It wasn't physical bullying, but it was psychological abuse. These people saw that I was weak and played on it. And it was going to stop.

If you've ever distanced yourself from a situation in which another woman deliberately prevented you from achieving your goals or made you feel put down and unworthy, you've probably come to terms with your own Queen Bees. If you're the aggressor and wake up each day contemplating how to maintain your position as queen of the hive, you may be ready to free yourself from anxiety-driven aggression and develop genuine power. Regardless of your situation, the following passage shows how the inherent strengths of women can be used to continually transform peer relationships.

The Art of Antagonism

OLGA DUGAN, PH.D., AND SHERRY AUDETTE MORROW

This spring, in the interest of nurturing our friendship (that is, finding an excuse for a "girls' night out"), we decided to nurture our creative interests and take an art class together. By the fifth week of our six-week drawing workshop, the two men and five women, including our instructor, had familiarized themselves with the relational dynamics of the studio setting. We artists had separated, both along gender lines and by attitude toward one another. This separation became especially clear during the fifth class, when the subtle tension of relational aggression rippled between two of our female classmates.

The men, Arney and Joe, whose age difference mirrored the differences between their drawing styles and subject matter, took tables at opposite corners of the studio, effecting detachment from each other and the rest of the group, while we occupied two tables along a side wall, sitting close enough to share our materials and the occasional word of encouragement without disturbing anyone's concentration. Our instructor, Bonnie, seemed to float about the classroom, simultaneously distant but connected as she entertained and instructed on topics varying from ways to create form over shape using light and shade to creative ways to dump undesirable wedding shower presents.

During the first two weeks, Reena and Micheline, or "Mitch," had migrated to what seemed to be front and center of the studio, their tables angled in a way that kept them from seeing each other's work, yet allowed them to share some "friendly" conversation. With pointed effort, they occasionally stood and crossed over the little chasm of floorboards between their tables to peek around each other's shoulder and critically eye the other's sketch pad. We had become accustomed to their wry exchanges, but one night their voices seemed pitched an octave higher than Madonna's soprano lilting from the radio, their words polite, their tone hostile.

Tossing auburn hair over a squared shoulder, Reena made what we thought was a rare effort to look Mitch in the eye as she described the Audi her husband "simply up and bought" for her "for no good reason." "I would have preferred a Land Rover," she added for good measure.

Mitch didn't bother to toss her ash-blonde curls; they just danced along the perfect lines of her gym-sculptured shoulders as she glared back at Reena. "My husband has this awkward way of buying me the most expensive and strangely timed presents, too," she claimed, bristling at the challenge of a verbal duel.

They continued sparring, comparing Stickley furniture, classy neighborhoods, and Reena's career as a freelance journalist to Mitch's dalliance as a landlord working out of the penthouse of her own apartment complex. Neither seemed able to best the other, until Reena changed her tactic.

"Have you ever eaten at Le Bec Fin?" Reena asked, inquiring about a restaurant the mayor and others among the city's glitterati frequented, but that she and her husband could afford only once or twice a month. Expressions of pretended disappointment, frustration, and, strangely, satisfaction flitted across Reena's face all at once. She was back on firm economic ground, familiar turf upon which she felt equal to Mitch.

Mitch affected concession and shook her head no, then, smiling broadly, asked Reena if she would join her for dinner, rattling off a list of expensive eateries she and her husband visited regularly. With a tight smile, Reena hesitantly accepted her offer. Disappointment flickered in her eyes. She could no longer deflect Mitch's parries without becoming openly rude. She had lost the verbal battle and thus was relegated to the subordinate position in what looked like a potentially ongoing acquaintanceship. In the silence that followed this wordplay, the two of us looked at each other, awed by, yet undeniably familiar with, what we had witnessed.

Relational aggression does exist between adult women on the community level. Reena and Mitch were part of the polite catfighting and one-upmanship in which women often feel compelled to engage. We have witnessed this type of behavior in all venues of both our personal and public lives and have been guilty of partaking in it ourselves. When we go into battle, our ammunition is our prestigious careers, our brilliant children, our better homes, cars, clothes, and vacations, even our illnesses and our shortcomings. As long as we have the biggest and the best, we can outshine everyone else and, in some twisted way, legitimize ourselves.

We recently went through a transformational period in our own twenty-year friendship, which made us especially sensitive to and grateful for the stark contrast between our behavior toward each other and that of the women in the studio. We had reached a point where the "things" of our lives had become more important than the friendship, trust, and communication that formed the foundation of our relationship.

We now share our thoughts and feelings at greater depth than we ever have, with consideration for the freedoms and limitations that characterize Sherry's lifestyle as a wife, mother, and editor of her own literary magazine along with the contrast of those that shape Olga's life as an English professor who is single and financially independent. We celebrate the similarities of our interests as writers, painters, and middle-aged women who have known each other since undergraduate school, but this did not come to us until we dropped the expectations of each other that kept us insecure, poised for disappointment, and always competing for a place in the other's life that we could not trust we already had.

Mitch did not invite Reena to dinner; she dared her, and Reena submitted to being bullied. Because of our experiences reconnecting, both through our art class and through our honest efforts to accept each other, we now understand that we must put aside our fear of failing to appear strong and independent in order to embrace the strength, self-sufficiency, and confidence that exist in both ourselves and the women who surround us—our mothers, our sisters, our friends, and our acquaintances. Women can and must learn alternative ways to foster relationships based on understanding, acceptance, and mutual respect for every woman's right to define what it means to be a woman in a community of women. Only then will we all be capable of reaching our full potential for self-exploration and for becoming true friends.

Olga and Sherry speak to the positive power of female connection, and describe why overcoming RA at all ages is a must. The gift of friendship and support they share is one every woman deserves.

CHAPTER 2

Why Women Aren't More Like Men

Can't a woman learn to use her head?
Why do they do everything their mothers do?
Why don't they grow up like their father instead?
—PROFESSOR HENRY HIGGINS, *MY FAIR LADY*

I frequently hear the question that since men are able to work together in competitive environments without taking things personally, why can't women? It's true that the concept of relational aggression is hard for many men to understand, but some basic gender differences explain the disconnect.

Female Facts

Some men use RA-type behaviors, but women are far more accomplished and familiar with this interaction style, perhaps because we are conditioned from birth to be more connection-focused. Consider how each of the following circumstances can place women of all ages at risk for RA:

- Boys learn to act out aggression at an early age in play and sports, while girls are discouraged from doing so.
- Girls who mature early feel less attractive than their peers; boys see their early development as an asset. Early on, girls come to prefer "sameness."

- Women are taught to work for the welfare of the group; men are taught to focus on personal achievement.

- Girls form friendships that mirror their relationships with their mothers, based on conformity rather than self-expression.

- Women of all ages develop their identities in the context of relationships. Who they are and how they feel about themselves often come from friendships and partnerships.

- Daughters, more than sons, are socialized to remain closer to their mothers. A woman carries out the majority of late-life caregiving for elders, even taking on the care of in-laws in place of her husband caring for his own parents.

While there are degrees of relevance to each circumstance, ultimately, women have a more social orientation than men. Historically, this female capacity to quickly establish and maintain connections has been essential in order for children to survive infancy.

Men and women also tend to deal with conflicts and differences in gender-specific ways: men want to fix problems rather than apologize, while women apologize and then fix; men tend to assume that a lack of complaint is the same as being satisfied, while women want direct praise; men often miss subtle meanings of conversations, while women intuit feelings into conversations; men focus on achieving outcomes, while women focus on forming relationships. In addition, men command more physical space than women. While not an ironclad rule for behavior, these descriptors may explain in part why RA is more prevalent in women, in settings from the play date to the powder room.

Sister Stress

Ironically, RA behaviors are counterintuitive to women's natural inclination to "tend and befriend." In 2000, Dr. Shelley Taylor, author of *The Tending Instinct*, reported on a study that shattered a long-held notion about the stress response. Previously, it was believed that in response to crises, men and women acted in the same way, gearing up for action and drawing on a powerful fight-or-flight response that dates back to prehistoric times. Not so, says Taylor. Her work suggests that female hormones such as oxytocin make women more likely to show a friend-seeking response during times of stress.

This is the tragedy of RA: it undermines the ability to relate and connect to others, which comes easier for most women than it does for men. These connections can sustain and support women through the worst situations.

The Beat Goes On

Although a few women told me otherwise, most women have been involved in some type of RA at one time or another in their lives. Many experience it every day, but there is a critical difference between isolated *incidents* and a relationally aggressive lifestyle. That is, the woman who occasionally acts as bully, in-betweener, or victim (and we all have the capacity to be each), isn't necessarily a Queen Bee, Middle Bee, or Afraid-to-Bee. Rather, a woman who is stuck in these behaviors, who can't or won't interact with others in any other way, is the woman who is cutting herself off from opportunities with her peers. The columnist Adriene Sere (www.saidit.org) makes a compelling argument for why women should preserve the unique bonds they share with one another in the following essay.

My Passion for Women
ADRIENE SERE

I tend to be a bit of a romantic, but I don't think it's an exaggeration to say that women sustain me. Women also enrage me, piss me off, betray me, but the bottom line is, women are the ones I can't live without. It is women who heal through meaningful connection, who fix through humble problem-solving, who bring joy through an honest presence. That's a generalization, of course. There are men who live their lives this way, and there are women who do quite well at manipulation and misuse of power. And then there are all the shades of grey. Still, my passion is for women.

My passion for women involves anger—at other women sometimes and at myself sometimes, too. Anger at women's protection of the powerful in exchange for a place with power. Anger at the misplaced rage, the inappropriate blame, the inappropriate forgiveness that follows.

I get angry when women refuse to stand by each other when the going gets tough. I expect more from women, because I depend more on women. I've been abandoned by women for those with more power, and I'll never forget what that's like. I must also admit that there have been times when I have been too afraid and confused to do the right thing. I know there has to be a place for forgiveness.

My passion for women is no less fueled by pride. I have seen women put each other first, take the side of justice, despite the risk, and I have seen the way everything changes—everything—when women are so connected to what's right that fear hardly seems to be a factor.

There are the women who, in the face of poverty, and violence, and media-brainwashing, manage to make cracks in the cement walls of oppression, seemingly with their bare fists. There are women who, against all odds, are healing, fixing, inventing, sustaining, thinking, challenging, and changing the world.

Everyone gets tired sometimes. Often we get scared and confused. We find ourselves repeating some despicable phrase or argument we never willingly allowed into our heads. We find ourselves hating our faces, hating our thighs, hating women who remind us of ourselves, hating the fight, hating defeat after defeat, too tired to remember all of the wins.

This is where passion comes in, passion to make good. One woman's passion is a lot. Women's collective passion transforms everything.

Friendsick

Despite the complex nature of our relationships, most women never stop striving for them. Certain phases of life, for example, motherhood, may limit our ability to be with friends, but we still long for a confidant. Studies have shown that a man's best friend is most often his spouse or romantic partner, but the same is not true for women. Men also seem to be able to set clearer boundaries for relationships: they recognize status and may struggle for dominance, but they tolerate a recognized hierarchy with relative equanimity.

Women's relationships with each other are both necessary and complex. Many of them are conditional, that is, established through children, spouses, or the workplace, thereby eliminating the element of choice. The involuntary nature of the following interactions may also create a context for RA:

- A child's birthday party list is carefully structured so children are or are not invited because of the relationships between their mothers.

- An opportunity for several coworkers and their spouses to visit a new restaurant arises and everyone is invited except Mike and his wife, Laura. Laura accidentally irritated the organizer of the event, the wife of Mike's boss, by interrupting her during a previous get-together.

- Melinda, a newlywed, is "forced" to join the church her husband's family has always attended. She is grouchy every Sunday and deliberately snaps at her sister-in-law, who has cheerfully adapted to the same situation.

The multidimensional life of the typical adult woman, who may be worker, mother, spouse, friend, sister, daughter, neighbor, and so on, can make it challenging to negotiate the nuances of relationships, as the following poem explicitly describes.

Best Friends
ANGELA EPPS

She is my friend. Children play together; Husbands talk cars
    forever.
She is my competition. I want my child to get what hers does.
My husband to be as attentive with his love.
She is my friend. Moves with fluid grace; can dance at any set
    pace.
She is my competition. Practicing to learn how she moves so.
I wish I could be like her, just let myself go.

She is my friend. A real natural beauty; Pampering is a loyal duty.

She is my competition. I strive to have her shape, her allure.

Dreaming men will notice me, not always her.

She is my friend. Trying on clothes; relying on what the other knows.

She is my competition. Looking better in all the outfits than I.

Feeling bad after every session, wanting to cry.

She is my friend. She consoles every tear; will echo every real fear.

She is my competition. I want her to think my life's just as good.

Tired of constantly hearing, "Well you should..."

She is my friend. We talk everyday; No matter there's nothing to say.

She is my competition. I envy the opportunities she's been given.

Never has to worry about how to keep living.

She is my friend. Sews the other's tattered seams, helps realize dreams.

She is my competition. Saying I have settled for less than deserved.

When she has her own issues hardly reserved.

She is my friend. Planting all the seeds; taking care of the other's needs.

She is my competition. Wanting more back than what I feel I get.

Leaving her side feeling less than adequate.

She is my friend. A woman refined. The best mother of all current time.

She is my competition. Making me want to be more feminine.

Feeling as if I lack what it means to be a woman.

She is my friend. Totally independent, no energy on all the critics, spent.

She is my competition. I crave for all that enlightening pride.

Not wanting, after a rejection, just to go and hide.

She is my friend. Advice galore, knowing whenever I need a shoulder.

She is my competition. If only I had unwavering confidence.

To truly believe my will and time were well spent.

She is my friend. No better one could be found; No secret is
unsound.
She is my competition. I long for achieving her kind of life.
Ending all my uncertainties and quelling all strife.
She is my friend. Every part of her I admire; All I am trying to
acquire.
She is my competition. She makes me, as a person, better.
Shows me parts of myself, knows me to the letter.
She is my friend. Helps me with the trait, Always before it was
too late.
She is my competition. Jealousy has before chased a friend.
She rises to the occasion and shows me different.
She is my friend. Finding the beauty to see, what I have missed
in me.
She is my competition. The best friend any girl could have.
My goal is to be as good to her as for me, she has.

Can't It Be a Relationship?

The author Christine Jahn was interested in a different aspect of
women's connections to one another. She solicited the opinions of
several women in an attempt to explore the contrary feelings of
competition and friendship women seem to experience. Note that
the women she included automatically responded to her questions
from a context of friendship, even though Christine clearly asked
them about relationships.

You Said It, Sister!

CHRISTINE JAHN

I've noticed that often the media portrays women at odds with
one another. I've had some enemies in my time who were
women, but on the whole I have been blessed with many
wonderful female friends and family members who are very
supportive of me, which led me to interview several women to
get their opinions on relationships between females.

I asked: How important is it to you to have good relationships with other women?

"Vital. I couldn't survive without my female friends," said
Michelle G. Ludlow of Australia.

Cindy Ricardo (no relation to Lucy) added, "For me, it is very important to be able to confide in and be understood and supported by other women."

The general consensus mirrored these opinions, but Dorothy Thompson, editor of *The Write Women*, injected, "I have always been more at home with 'the guys.' That is, until I suffered a breakup with my boyfriend. Then, my girlfriends rallied around me and nurtured me until I could get back on my feet again."

When asked who their top two female supporters are, the women all had similar answers. The first person on most of their "Wonderful Women" lists was their mothers. My list was no different.

The next most important female in the women's lives was usually a sister or a best friend. My friend Melissa and I have shared many serious conversations, and we've also laughed together for hours. Conquering similar problems made us kindred spirits.

Jeanni Brosius, a syndicated columnist and author, said of her mother and sister, "They have always been there and have always supported my life choices."

Most of the comments suggested these women were good friends because they didn't judge. I don't have a biological sister, but my sister-in-law, Tamatha, is a wonderful friend to me. She loves my brother and his entire family, including me, and we love her in return. She gives great advice and always reminds me to "breathe." I might forget if she wasn't around.

Next on the survey was, "What is it about these two relationships that you feel enriches your life?"

Most of the women said, very emphatically, trust.

Connie E. Curry, a freelance writer, said that besides her sister and best friend, next on her list is: "Wonderful friends I relate to through e-mail and my writers group." She expressed how it is funny to feel such a bond and never to have met. I knew what she meant because of my Internet buddy, Bonnie. We've never met in person, but I feel I know her better than most people I have met. She is a fellow writing soul and very understanding.

When asked if they think they can have the same supportive relationships with men, in a nonsexual manner, the women's responses were mixed. Susan said that she does think it is possible, but she sees "the potential for this evolution more in my daughter's generation."

Connie added, "The friendship of a man is different, because he cannot relate to a woman like another woman can."

Jeanni disagreed by saying, "Men are less judgmental of women than other women are and less competitive."

Jackie Horn thinks that it's hard to have a relationship with a man who has a significant other, because it could cause problems for the woman in his life and vice versa. I tend to agree. I don't want my husband to have a really close relationship with any females besides our family members and myself.

The final question was about how the media portrays female relationships. Does it encourage or discourage women supporting women? Michelle replied that in Australia the media handles it in a very encouraging manner. "New York Vicky" responded, "A little of both, but the catfights and sickness that goes on in soap operas, along with the fake hand holding and support, is detrimental to the women who watch." She said there are shows that are very encouraging, but "we need more."

Bobbie Baxter, who operates a Web site for women, had this to say in response to my interview questions: "Only other women can relate to how we feel and process information, and what we encounter in life. Women are very complex and multilayered. We're delicious creatures who lead with our hearts and emotions. Men can love us, try to relate to and understand us, but only women seem to be able to truly understand and support us in the way we understand best.

"The five women in my healing circle are as close as sisters to me. The bonds are so strong between us all that it doesn't matter what kind of mood we're in or if one of us is having a bad day. All that matters is the glorious bond we share."

"I think it (the media) used to discourage support (of women) but that's changing now, thankfully. We're seeing more and more powerful female roles and friends in movies and TV shows. The jealous catfights are being replaced with strong women fighting side by side."

Bobbie also added, "I really enjoy a friend who disagrees with me and isn't afraid to tell me when she does. If my friend always thinks the same as me, one of us isn't necessary."

Wounded by Our Own

As the previous essay highlighted, women can provide unprecedented support for one another during times of sorrow and celebration. Unlike men, however, who are inclined not to aggress against men in general or their friends in particular, women do both, as the following essay shows.

Relational Aggression and Sex on the College Campus: Why Some Women Are Sluts

CAITLIN' J. PAUSE'

On a recent episode of *Real Time* on HBO, Bill Maher stated that the defense of Kobe Bryant was going to try to limit the number of women on the jury. Maher commented that the apparent reason for a masculine panel was that women were thought to be harder on the victim in sexual assault cases. Maher stated that the defense claimed that women would often think, "Well, I wouldn't have put myself in that position. She should have known better."

Watching his commentary brought up reminders of past experiences I encountered with women within the college community. All of my experiences with relational aggression have been based on beliefs about sexual behaviors and practices.

When I was an undergraduate at a large university based in a small, southern town, I participated in a peer education group called The Network. We would go into the college classrooms, dorms, and organizations and give presentations about health-related issues (sex, alcohol, drugs, etc.). One of my frequent programs was on acquaintance rape. The presentation consisted of looking over how rape has been dealt with in the past, examining common elements that lead to acquaintance rape, and ending with discussions based on scenarios presented to the students, who had been broken up into groups. In each scenario, an acquaintance rape would occur, and we would ask the students to rate the situation from 1 (representing "not rape") to 5 (representing "rape").

I was always surprised (even after several occasions) at how hostile the young women in the groups were toward the women in the scenarios. Very rarely did the young women feel that the situation ranked anything higher than a 2, and they often had commentary to back up their claim. One particular scenario had a woman inviting a man to her apartment, eating dinner with him on the floor, kissing and fondling him, and then allowing him to undress her before she said no four times. Many young women expressed that the woman in this scenario was a "slut" and "definitely had it coming." One young lady commented, "She had to have known what was going to happen. Only an idiot would not have known." Often women suggested the only reason the woman said no was to play "hard to get" or keep her appearance as a lady.

I received another surprise after I began working on my masters degree at another university. I was studying the high-risk sexual behaviors of undergraduate college students and interviewed fourteen men and twelve women about their attitudes toward sexual activity as well as their own sexual behaviors. Of these twelve women, two had very strong negative feelings regarding sexually active women, even though both of them were sexually active.

One girl, who was referred to as Susan in my writing, stated: "I know it sounds bad, but when girls are buying condoms, it just seems kinda skanky to me." Another woman, Stephanie, commented that she was cautious about the men she slept with because "you don't know what the hell these people have around here, you know. You have so many women around here just smashing it up with anybody." One of the men in my study, Anthony, remarked, "My mom talked to me, and she said you can't trust women. She said that they will lie to you, they'll tell you that they are on birth control, and the next thing you know you are a dad."

I found these responses from undergraduates very disconcerting. In the case of Anthony, it was his mother who warned him about sexually active women and what great liars they were. The two young women who responded with hostility and negativity obviously distrusted women as a sexually active whole, even though they themselves fell into the group they were stereotyping. These perceptions that women are expected to be "sexual gatekeepers" bode badly for an RA-free future.

When beliefs and values that support negativism come from within the ranks of women, whether from mother to son or young woman to young woman, it deals an especially damaging blow and perpetuates stereotypes about female relationships. After reading Caitlin's essay, it's not hard to understand why sayings like "women are their own worst enemies" gain credibility.

Friend, Foe, or Not Quite Either?

Women may have a natural inclination to plunge into, wrestle with, and agonize over relationships that inadvertently trigger aggressive exchanges. The Queen Bee has learned to be constantly on the offense in her interactions with peers, launching preemptive strikes that she believes will protect or further her interests. She trusts no one and prevents peers from glimpsing the real person underneath her aggressive mask. The Middle Bee finds herself in a similar bind but is much less overt in her efforts to establish herself. She may have learned to be subtle in the messages she gives others, or she may secretly straddle the fence between aggression and passivity, combining both attitudes or vacillating between them. The Afraid-to-Bee desperately wants to make connections that will empower and help rather than hurt her, but lacks the confidence or skill to do so. This makes her fearful and uncertain of just about every woman she encounters.

Add to these behaviors a tendency to see relationships as either-or and confusion over what it means to be friends with a woman (is she your closest confidant, fiercest competitor, chief supporter, or all three?), and it's not surprising that tension occurs. Women understand this, even if they don't approve of it.

"I grew up with all sisters, so I know how it goes. Men have buddies, they have coworkers, and they have just guys in their lives. Women don't have any neutral women in their lives. It's just the way we are. Either we like or we don't—no in between," says Rita, one of six siblings. Maybe her theory is the soundest of all.

CHAPTER 3

Big Bullies and Other Aggressive Types

The Queen Bee

Do not start with me. You will not win.

—A BUMPER STICKER

Queen Bees are at the top of the RA food chain, exerting their authority over all others and jealously protecting their power. What makes a Queen Bee? Consider the words of Teresa, a college junior, who reflects back on high school:

> My best friend was a Queen Bee in middle school. She deliberately humiliated other girls for the clothes they wore, their hair styles, or the shapes of their bodies. Lots of times she'd draw me into the schemes she dreamed up, getting me to pass hurtful notes to others or convincing me to stand by her as she blasted another girl. But then one day she turned on me, supposedly her very best friend. She was talking to a boy I liked, and when I came up to them she said, "Terri, you need to get some new clothes. You've been wearing that shirt since fifth grade!" It might sound like a little thing, but to me it was the ultimate humiliation—her smirk, the way she nudged the boy, and the tone of her voice. Then right before we graduated from high school, we happened to volunteer on a project together. I kept my distance, but then she told me she was so sorry for how she had behaved all those years ago. She said, "Terri, I'm really different now, because I realize how mean I

was." At first I wasn't sure, but then I gave her a chance, and I saw that she had made a decision to be different. We ended up going away to college together, and now we're really close. I think the way she was when she was younger made her decide never to act like that again. I've seen it go the other way, too, though. The Queen Bee of the boardroom was hatched in the locker room of high school.

While not every mean girl continues such behavior as an adult, the seeds of this relationship style are most often planted in the tender middle school years. None of the stories I received described an adolescent of integrity who turned into an aggressive adult.

Could It Be You?

Bullies rarely recognize themselves as such, which is part of the problem. The reporter Tammy Jordon described a new makeover program for women managers identified as "bully bosses" "Bully Bosses Find Their Gentler Side" (*Atlanta Journal and Constitution*, September 2001). The women encouraged to enroll by their superiors described themselves as "take charge," "too direct," "need[ing] help with interpersonal skills," "high achiever," and "[having] ultra-high expectations." None thought they were aggressive or viewed their behavior as hurtful, but clearly others did and guided them to help.

Many Queen Bees don't recognize the aggressive nature of their behavior. The following questions can help you evaluate behaviors you may rely on that are common to bullies:

1. Am I more likely to be irritated than intrigued by other women?

2. Do I use defamatory language when I think about other women?

3. Am I always in charge, calling the shots, making the plans, and leading the show, without asking for input from others?

4. Do I cycle through coworkers or friends quickly?

5. Do I lack meaningful relationships with women?

6. Am I rarely asked to do things with other women, whether it's going to lunch at work or a leisure activity at home?

7. Do I constantly think about how I will attain or maintain a position of power at work or in the community?

8. Do other women seem to avoid me?

9. Have I forgotten to apologize when I knew I was wrong, believing it didn't really matter?

10. Do I shut out women who give me feedback on my performance or behavior?

11. Is being the best, no matter what the cost, all-important to me?

12. Have I ever deliberately schemed to exclude or sabotage another woman?

13. Does my relationship style intimidate other women?

14. Is it hard for me to feel close to other women?

15. If I hear gossip about another woman, do I repeat it?

If you answered yes to many of these questions, you most likely are engaging in aggressive behaviors that alienate and even hurt those around you. Perhaps it takes this kind of tally to sensitize us to the ways in which all of us, at some point in time, may take advantage of and harm other women. This is a realization that can be devastating. Often, women who come to understand that their actions have been not only unhelpful but destructive are overcome by remorse, as happened to Leah, a "go-to" girl who climbed the career ladder by exploiting her female colleagues.

Leah admits that she stole other women's ideas, undermined their abilities, and openly professed a preference for hanging out with the guys at the firm where she worked. When Leah developed a rare form of skin cancer at age thirty, it was her female colleagues who stepped up to help her, providing both emotional and tangible forms of support.

Now Leah, recovering from her illness, is ashamed of her previous behavior. "I can't believe what a bitch I was," she says. "The women I worked with had more integrity in their thumbs than I did in my whole body. I've apologized to every one of them."

Liz, a woman in Australia, shared with me the reasons behind her past aggressive behavior and revealed an incident where she "squared off" with another bully.

I am a very strong woman, the first of seven children in a poor Irish family where abuse was common from an early age. As the oldest, I became a surrogate wife and parent, and, as a result, my own behavior was often very strong, aggressive, and occasionally violent—behaviors I modified as I learned to identify triggers and deal with my own issues.

I continue to be a very strong individual, less given to intimidating behavior. However, if it were not for my strength of character and sheer bloody determination, I would not be alive to tell my story.

Being friendly and optimistic by nature, I have little difficulty fitting into most environments or engaging in conversation with most people. However, I can and do withdraw from others who are of an aggressive or intimidating nature, such as one of the members at the gym, who I will call Ann.

Despite no conversation between us (she refuses to be engaged), I have sensed a jealousy and resentment from Ann, particularly when we have been in close quarters in the locker room.

One morning, another member offered his treadmill to me when he finished his workout. I gladly accepted, not realizing Ann was pumping away on her bike waiting for a treadmill to become free. At the same time, Lynn, a member of the staff who has also become a friend, was speaking to me as I began my workout. Both of us were enjoying our usual girl talk, making arrangements for our regular coffee catch-up.

Ann was so incensed when I jumped on the treadmill that she verbally abused Lynn, decrying the staff and lack of system for the use of the equipment in the mornings. Refusing to direct her anger at me, she screamed at Lynn, demanding she do something and glaring at the fellow who gave me the treadmill. I had not realized my transgression, but I sensed it was me that she really was angry with, so I turned up the speed on the treadmill to escape her anger.

Later, Lynn and I laughed uproariously over coffee, as Lynn had no idea why I was running like a bat out of hell on the treadmill. She did tell me Ann is given to violent behavior, to the extent of threatening another member with hand weights on one occasion. I daresay Ann senses that, despite my friendly manner, she would be no match for me as I would not tolerate such behavior. However, unlike in my earlier years, my tongue now is a far more dangerous weapon than any dumbbells she may wish to heave in my direction.

I have great empathy for Ann, recognizing that certain behaviors are the result of other issues, such as being victimized in the past. However, I believe that at some point in our lives, we need to be accountable for our behavior and accept responsibility for our own recovery, as I have done.

She's All That . . . Isn't She?

Aggressive women who bully their way through life appear to have it all together. They don't hesitate to take action, nor do they consider the consequences of their verbal grenades or subtle sabotages, which are often considerable. Yet just like their adolescent counterparts, those who rely on cruel behaviors to get their way are not so secure underneath. If anything, they are terrified, threatened, and on the verge of collapse. Consider a recent book, *Same Game, Different Rules: How to Get Ahead without Being a Bully Boss, Ice Queen, or Ms. Understood* by the counselor Jean Hollands. In her program for women executives, Hollands coaches bullies on how to cry and describes the "internal mush" that each outwardly aggressive woman harbors and needs to be free of.

The following story illustrates the insecurities of aggressive women well.

Bully Boss
CAROL HOLMAN

I was a professional with a master's degree, but for nine painful years I worked under a female supervisor I now recognize was a bully. This woman was clever enough to look good to her employers. In fact, they named a center after her when she retired.

I'm convinced that bullies are emotionally damaged people

unable to function rationally in a logical world. Unfortunately, understanding that may or may not help a subordinate survive working under a bully.

The characteristics of the female bullies I observed were these:

- Must be in control
- Won't admit they made a mistake despite logical and reasonable rebuttals
- Have an uncanny ability to look good to peers and superiors
- Intimidate through belittling, undermining the self-confidence of the women they supervise and establishing themselves as the superior human beings
- May single out only one individual to hassle, making it difficult for superiors to recognize what they're doing
- Display arrogance and see themselves as above the rules, while paradoxically, a competent subordinate may be seen as very threatening
- Will begin to bully male peers as well as women subordinates, if their behavior is not stopped by their superiors
- May turn on subordinates who support them.

If you're singled out for hassling, your work life can be difficult in the extreme. To avoid becoming a target, it's important to identify a bully boss quickly. Then I suggest applying these behaviors with her:

- Avoid acting timid or overly confident. Bullies love to squash confident as well as timid women.

- Recognize that you cannot convince her through logic that two plus two equals four. Don't even go there. Remember, she cannot admit to having made mistakes.

- Never upstage her. This is very dangerous. It threatens her delusions of grandeur.

- Avoid defending yourself. If reprimanded, give in gracefully to her "superiority" with phrases such as "You may be right," "I didn't realize that," "I see what you mean," "I'll follow your lead," and so on. She's looking for someone she can bully, and when you resist, you give her the green light to beat you down.

- Don't look her in the eye if she terrifies you. Instead, create the illusion of looking her in the eye by focusing your gaze in the space between her eyes. Try it with a friend or spouse. It works.

- Maintain an employee-boss relationship. Don't try to be a friend, because you set yourself up for personal as well as on-the-job betrayal.

- Keep notes at home of your encounters with her if you're already the target of a bully boss. Write them down when they occur, noting the time, the date, and the place of the encounter. Log her exact words.

- Check for contract violations, especially in the area of evaluations, if your position is covered by a contract. Check out the labor laws in regard to your job. Seek union or employee association counsel if available. Arrive with your encounter notes and your contract in hand.

- Ask yourself how important this job is for you. How much bullying can you tolerate emotionally and physically? Do you have other options such as a transfer, or do you need to find work elsewhere?

You may need to do as my friend Janet did. She was a well-regarded, credentialed school nurse who had worked for twelve years in a district. A new boss, a woman bully, was hired. Under her, the school nurse position became alarmingly stressful and unsatisfying. At fifty-five, Janet could retire with a small pension, so on her fifty-fourth birthday she enrolled quietly in weekend massage therapy classes. She celebrated her fifty-fifth birthday with early retirement and a new profession.

Janet is happy. Her former boss was fired after over-reaching herself by bullying male peers, but by that time the district had lost several valuable nurses. None chose to be rehired. They had a right to a life. A life free from being bullied.

The guidelines offered by Carol Holman give insight and direction to all women who have felt trapped in a work situation with a hurtful, aggressive boss. For those who find they have many (if not all) of the traits attributed to "bully bosses," the story can serve as a catalyst for change.

The Making of a Bee

Sometimes the Queen Bee of today may have been yesterday's Afraid-to-Bee victim, responding now with a furious buzz instead of a whimper when she feels threatened by a peer. In other cases, she may be a lifelong Queen Bee who believes that aggression is the answer to every challenge. Aggressive women often act on perceptions rather than reality, assuming certain things about their prey that might not be true. In the same way, victims of the attack may search for flaws in their own behavior that explain the assault.

"I kept wondering what I did to upset her so," Wendy, a bewildered victim said, recounting a year as a graduate student in which her faculty office mate turned predatory. "The more I tried to work things out, the angrier she got. Finally I asked others if I was taking up too much space or somehow irritating this other woman. 'Nah,' they told me, 'she has a reputation for eating teaching assistants alive.'" Despite this assurance, Wendy's time as a student was made miserable by the continued sabotage of an older woman who could have, in other circumstances, been a mentor.

Sometimes, Queen Bees are simply misinformed. In an odd paradox, today's women are often encouraged to "go for the gold," but to do it like a lady. The words "assertive" and "aggressive" are used interchangeably, as in the comment made by a mother: "I told my daughter that she should never let anyone get the upper hand. She should make sure she takes care of herself in every situation. You know, be assertive."

The Big Sell

The story of Jean Racine, the bobsledder who switched partners shortly before her competition in the 2002 Winter Olympics, is a good example of this paradoxical logic. When Racine made the decision to replace Jen Davidson, her teammate, the media came down hard with harsh headlines about "Mean Jean," and cruel commentary on her ruthlessness. Meanwhile, the same behavior in men is regularly condoned if not admired.

From an early age, women are given messages that encourage

them to use undermining and hurtful behaviors with one another. Products are sold to make one woman more beautiful than all the others. Television shows and movies urge women to compete with one another in openly aggressive ways, the more extreme the better. One makeover show features women only, and encourages them to vie against one another in a posttransformation beauty contest. On television sitcoms men have buddies; if a woman has friends, they are likely to be men: Elaine from *Seinfeld* and Diane from *Cheers* had close relationships with men but conflicted ones with women. The primetime prizewinning dramedy *Desperate Housewives* capitalizes on this kind of no-holds-barred aggression among stay-at-home wives and mothers.

And when women are enemies? One only has to watch enough football to catch a commercial where bikinied babes mud wrestle over a man to understand that message—and the fact that perpetuating the public image of female aggression is a serious marketing tool.

In the years to come these media influences are likely to produce an even more aggressive generation of women, if current trends are accurate. A 2002 article by Bryan Rourke in the *Providence Journal* discussed the connection between media messages and escalating female aggression, noting that "females, according to the U.S. Department of Justice, now account for 25 percent of juvenile arrests for violent crime. And since 1981, their rate of arrest for violent crimes has increased 129 percent." Dr. Deborah Prothrow-Stith, director of the Harvard University of Public Health, said in the article, "We are surprised they're girls and their behaviors are aggressive. There are more surprises to come."

It's not just violence in music, movies, TV programs and video games that's a problem, Prothrow-Stith asserts: it's the accumulation and celebration of it all. And it's not just the way women are depicted in the media, but the way they solve problems that is troubling. "We teach violence," she said. "It's a learned behavior." For the next generation of young women who haven't developed the ability to be critical consumers of the media, these messages may be taken as a sanction of aggression.

The Bottom Line

Women who rely excessively on bullying behaviors to get their way cause problems for themselves, creating tension and havoc at home, at work, and at play. This is not to suggest that passivity is the preferred course of action since it, too, has consequences.

The challenge Queen Bees have never quite mastered is to differentiate between assertiveness and aggression, just as her Afraid-to-Bee counterpart struggles to voice her opinions in an appropriate and effective way. The bottom line, and an easy rule to follow, is: if your behavior hurts or takes advantage of another, it needs to change.

CHAPTER 4

From Mild to Bad and In Between

The Middle Bee

I didn't know what to do. If I spoke up, she'd turn on me,
but it was miserable to watch her publicly destroy Wanda,
like it was fun for her. Finally, I had enough, and
I said, "What's going on here?" That changed the
whole dynamic. I just wish I'd spoken up sooner.

—A WOMAN IN BETWEEN WHO IS A FRIEND OF BOTH A
BULLY AND A VICTIM ON THE SCHOOL BOARD

In adolescence, the girl in between an aggressor and a victim is often called a bystander because she watches as a bully Queen Bee inflicts hurt. Underlying the seemingly passive stance of bystanders is a fear of being targeted if they speak up or tension over being caught in the middle. For adult women, the middle role is not so one-dimensional or easily explained. Rather, the Middle Bee is much more active, often making it possible for the Queen Bee to maintain her position at the top of the hive.

If you wonder about your Middle Bee potential, ask yourself these questions:

1. Am I always thinking of ways to stay in the middle of a controversy between other women or do I naturally find myself there and enjoy it?

2. Do I plan to tell certain women information I've heard, but withhold it from others?

3. Is there a Queen Bee I keep indebted to me because I provide her with regular updates on rumors that involve her?

4. Do I keep some women down by cultivating a Queen Bee and influencing her opinions?

5. Is my day spent obtaining and sharing information about other women, even if the information isn't necessarily true?

6. When other women confide in me, do I sometimes break their confidences because their secrets are too irresistible not to pass on?

7. Do I watch a Queen Bee intimidate someone and fail to walk away?

8. Am I the person who "controls" the information flow in my work, neighborhood, school, community, or organization?

9. Would other women think of me as the Queen Bee's "right hand?"

10. Do I use my abilities to control rumors and gossip as a way to connect with other women?

Stuck in the Middle with You

As a woman matures, she is less likely to stand by and watch another woman be teased or tormented. Instead, when interactions become uncomfortable, the adult woman will be more likely than an adolescent to flee or distance herself, as the following story demonstrates.

Cyclone Season
CONNIE WEBER

I teach children with severe special needs, a profession in which care and nurturing are at the heart of everything I do. With as much love, concern, and stamina as we can muster, my female assistants and I guide our students toward productive, meaningful lives. It's hard but rewarding work. This year, by some fluke, all our students are girls. We began the year like sorority sisters, enjoying our femininity and treating our girls like princesses. We laughed, sang, talked about shopping and clothes, and indulged ourselves in being female.

Then suddenly, in February, a cataclysmic storm hit. Without warning it seems, our camaraderie was ravaged. One of my assistants, Marge, began a campaign to undermine the integrity of Sandy, another assistant. Rude comments, said under Marge's breath at first, chilled the air. She openly ignored anything the other women said and blamed Sandy for every difficulty we had. Marge's disgust for Sandy pelted us all, like driving rain. Soon, dark clouds enveloped the classroom and the air was so thick with loathing that none of us could breathe freely.

Marge crept slowly around the edges of Sandy's credibility and shredded it, bit by bit. She spent weeks talking secretly to other people in the school. To anyone who would listen, she made up stories about Sandy and lied about difficulties that we allegedly were having in the classroom. Sandy's reputation has been damaged to a point where it may never be repaired.

As I watched the scenes between these two women unfold, I was astounded. One day there was nothing wrong, and the next, the entire basis of our working relationship had washed away. The storm had been brewing for some time in Marge's mind, but it was far out to sea, so none of us were aware of it. When it finally hit shore, it hit with the force of a category five hurricane. The storm whipped all around Sandy and tried to pull her off her foundation. The rest of us were lashed by waves of anger and resentment.

For Sandy, it was a double whammy. She was on the mend from devastating personal problems when Hurricane Marge descended without warning. Before that, Sandy had actually trusted and looked up to her aggressor. Sandy tried asking Marge what exactly she had done to cause this wave of hostility, but the response was only that they were just too different and couldn't work together.

Picking through the rubble of what is left of our work environment, I can see some clues. I remember the comments dropped casually, before I knew there was a tempest approaching. Bits and pieces fit together now, like the shards of glass from a broken picture window: Marge telling me Sandy didn't need this job and that she really ought to quit to take care of her personal life; comments relating to a friend who Marge felt would be a good match to work in our classroom; cryptic phone calls to administrators at opportune times while I was in earshot; carefully crafted information, related at just the right time.

Like the survivors of a devastating storm waiting for a check from the insurance company, we're waiting for the relief of summer vacation, but it makes me wonder—what happens next year? Marge's accusations and dissatisfaction have called everyone's integrity into question. How will we rebuild? Can we possibly salvage anything from this experience? Who will survive the devastation and return in the fall?

Weber fits the definition of an in-betweener who finds herself stuck in the middle of a conflict she neither precipitated nor wants to see continue. However, the Middle Bee's position of noninvolvement can be used unwittingly to turn her into an accomplice, as evidenced in the following story.

A Gentle Nudge?

CINDY ROBERT

"So, what did you think of the movie? I loved it, though personally, I think she should have gone with him, but hey, I'm a romantic at heart!" I said, as my friend Wendy and I walked out to the parking lot.

Ignoring my question, Wendy said, "See, I was right! You didn't even want to go out tonight. If I hadn't kept at you, you'd be at home torturing yourself with thoughts about your ex and his latest fling. Isn't that Robin over there? I need to talk to her. Robin, over here," Wendy called and motioned with her arm..

"Oh, hi, ladies. I didn't know you were here," Robin said, joining us. "Did you enjoy the movie? I thought it was—"

Wendy cut her off, evidently not wanting to hear her review of the movie either. "Have you sent your story in yet, Robin?"

"Not yet, but . . . "

"Not yet? The deadline is less than two weeks away. If you don't mail it out soon, it won't reach them in time, and you'll be disqualified." Wendy explained this as though to a small child.

"I just wanted to give it one more go over," Robin answered, as though she suddenly were one.

"One more 'go over'? You mean like the last contest I told you to enter? Remember what happened with that one? Do you?"

"I, uh, missed the cutoff time," Robin answered, now not only a child, but a naughty one.

"Yes, you did. I spend a lot of my time and energy finding writing contests that I think would be good matches for you, that I think you have a good shot at. I don't know, maybe I'm just wasting my time and shouldn't bother."

"No, Wendy, don't say that. I appreciate it. Really, I do. I'll get moving," Robin said, taking an involuntary step backward.

"Then prove it!" Wendy countered, moving toward her.

I stood my ground, but stared at the asphalt and kept silent.

"I'll get it out in tomorrow's mail. I promise. I'll get it all addressed, stamped, and ready to go tonight, just as soon as I get home." Looking at her watch, Robin continued, "I really have to run. I'll see you both later."

"I'll phone you tomorrow morning to remind you, just in case you forget, " Wendy called at her retreating back.

"Bye, Robin. Be careful going home." I waved, waiting until Robin was out of earshot before turning back to Wendy. "I know you two have been friends for ages, but don't you think you are being awfully hard on her? She is a grown woman, in case you hadn't noticed."

"Robin has talent, and more importantly, she has dreams. She wants to be an author, has ever since I've known her. Unfortunately, she has a fear of failure. Robin thinks it is better to keep a dream than to fail at it and have no dream at all."

"And you've taken it upon yourself to see that she succeeds?"

"No, that part is up to her. I just want make sure she tries."

"So you push her?"

"I like to think of it more as a gentle nudge. Now, let's go get a cup of coffee. There is something I want to talk to *you* about."

Cindy's story is a classic example of how women can be drawn into the Middle Bee role without realizing it. In other cases, Middle Bees are less innocent about participating in a hurtful exchange. While there can be only one supreme Queen Bee aggressor, her authority can be abetted by malicious Middle

Bees, who operate covertly as accomplices. Consider the following scenario.

Honey-Dipped Claws
ALEXANDRA BOURQUIN

The scene is a suburban tennis club:

"You are such a godsend, Jane, making up the schedule for us, summer after summer. It's so much work."

"Yeah, Betty, it's always a pain figuring out the partnerships. This year was especially bad, because Sue refuses to play with Pam. Pam doesn't know this, and Sue doesn't want me to tell her. So now I suppose Pam will end up bitching at me, because she'll think it's my fault she never gets to play with Sue. Women!"

"You poor sweetie. Trust Sue to be two-faced about the whole thing. You know, I was thinking, maybe you should let somebody else have a go at being captain—give yourself a break from the hassles."

Jane chose to ignore this. "That's not the only problem," she said. "Carolyn's been playing first doubles for years, and she's used to being Queen Bee. She's gonna be royally pissed when I move her down to second. I have to do it though. She's gotten slow since she had that knee surgery."

"You want me to do it?"

"What, tell her?"

"No. You want me to play first doubles?"

Jane avoided eye contact. "Er . . . no. Thought I'd have Karen do it."

"You think Karen's better than me?"

Jane sighed. "Look, Betty, I don't want to hurt your feelings, but we need somebody younger."

"Fine."

But it was obviously not fine at all, and Jane, anxious to change the subject, pasted on an encouraging smile,

"Our team should do well this year, after all those lessons we took over the winter."

"Hmm, yeah. Um . . . I've been talking to the girls . . ."

"Oh?"

"Well, we're all wondering . . . what about Helen? She didn't take the lessons."

"So?"

"We were thinking maybe she should join a different group. If she can't keep up, she'll drag the whole team down."

"She'll be fine."

"Some of the girls aren't happy."

"We can't drop her. I don't think she could afford the lessons."

"We have to think of the team, Jane."

"If she goes, I go."

"Well, you've done a wonderful job over the years, Jane, and I'm sure the girls will want to give you a little farewell party. How's next Thursday?"

Alexandra's description of two women disguising their malice as good intentions is another way Middle Bees facilitate aggression. Women like these tennis players sweetly slash away at the reputations of others yet can still claim in-between status because they didn't directly launch an attack.

Sometimes the Middle Bee gossip circle is more like a merry-go-round: as one woman leaves, another replaces her to whisper about the person who just departed. Mary, who witnessed such behavior, commented, "It doesn't matter who is there or who isn't, someone gets trashed. I'm sure it happens to me, too." Trudy, a mom who had to leave a play date session early with her children wondered, "Am I the person those other moms will be talking about as soon as I'm gone?"

A feeling of importance, the desire for excitement, and a penchant for drama are all reasons women give for engaging in campaigns like the one just described. Because the aggression is subtle, conversation is a powerful weapon that can be used in a variety of ways: changing the tone of voice or facial expressions to alter the meaning of the words, withholding important details, and exaggerating or embellishing content. All these tactics are the arsenal of the Middle Bee.

Pick a Little, Talk a Little

While a Queen Bee won't hesitate to attack directly, gossip and rumors are the ammunition Middle Bees use against other women. Their assaults can succeed, however, only if other women relay the messages that have come their way. While passing on a spicy tidbit of information may seem both common and innocuous, when the content is hurtful, the Middle Bee becomes an aggressor in her own right. Often this happens inadvertently. Imagine that the following scenario happens to you:

In the grocery store, you run into Lynn, a woman with whom you have shared car pools and child care. You like Lynn, but she is a notorious busybody who claims to know what is going on with everyone in your neighborhood, at the school your children attend, and in your husband's place of employment. As you stop your carts and chat in the aisle, Lynn tells you the latest rumor about Carol Martin, the school superintendent, who has been catching a lot of flak for her leadership style. According to Lynn, there was an incident involving Carol and a male student. Carol is the first woman to become a superintendent in your community. She attends your church and is known to you, so of course you are interested in what Lynn has to say.

After a few minutes of talk, you tear yourself away from Lynn and dash to the drugstore to pick up a prescription. You find yourself waiting in line with Barb, another mom from your neighborhood with whom you are acquainted.

"So what do you think about the latest problem Carol Martin's run into?" Barb asks, raising her eyebrows suggestively.

What do you do? As a woman who has the potential to pass on Lynn's juicy version of the facts, you are caught in the middle, torn between wanting to discuss what you've just heard but hesitant to spread a rumor that could be very damaging to a woman you know. Every day, the volume of information that comes our way requires this kind of decision making.

Given the option of passing on a particular bit of gossip, the Middle Bee will always choose to continue the rumor mill, spreading information guaranteed to be hurtful and sometimes even adding a little malicious twist of her own. When confronted with a situation like the one just described, ask yourself what your motivations are for sharing the latest "news" with another woman.

Malicious Middle Bees

Unlike adolescents, who often get caught between an aggressor and a victim, grown women sometimes deliberately place themselves there. This is the malicious version of the Middle Bee, who not only passes on gossip and rumors but tries to perpetuate aggression, constantly working undercover to create a context ripe for conflict. Although she has no inherent power, the Middle Bee creates some for herself by keeping bullies and victims isolated and selectively feeding the Queen Bee information calculated to incite her anger. As a master of behind-the-scenes antagonism, the Middle Bee ensures that bullying will continue without ever being accused of being directly involved.

Consider the following story, told to me by a woman who experienced the vicious nature of the Middle Bee.

In my office, my supervisor, Andrea, is generally negative to everyone except a woman I'll call Tina. A few years ago, Andrea seemed to single me out for overt hostility. Everything I did was wrong. I couldn't file, make coffee, or answer the phone the way she wanted me to, even though I'd been doing this stuff the same way for years and never had a bad performance review. The nonstop bullying got to me, and I repeatedly broke down to my husband. Finally, he said enough was enough and encouraged me to hand in my resignation, which I did.

Andrea came to me in tears, begging to know why I would leave. I was stunned, but knowing that she would never be able to bully me again I outlined the behaviors she was using that led me to resign. She was devastated and said that contrary to what I thought, she admired me a great deal because I was taking college classes to better myself while caring for my ill mother.

Andrea asked me to give her another chance, so I said I would (in our small town, it's hard to find jobs). I then began to be aware that Tina was constantly buzzing around the office, going from desk to desk and talking to each of us, then running into Andrea's office. Tina spent more time away from her desk than at it.

Given my new relationship with Andrea, I went to her and expressed my concern about Tina feeding her information on the rest of us. I shared my observations, and after a moment of reflection, Andrea admitted I might be right. Later that day, she took me aside and said she realized Tina *had* told her things about me, such as that I hoped to take her job, and that I criticized other women who did not care for their parents in late life (Andrea's father had passed away in another state the year before).

It was my turn to think back, and I realized I had talked to Tina about those things, but not in the way she suggested. I had said I wanted to take classes because I'd never been able to before, and when she asked if I hoped for a promotion, I said someday, sure, I would like to try something different. As for my mother, I had remarked to a group during lunch that I felt fortunate to be able to take care of my mother, because not everyone had this option. Somehow Tina twisted that into criticism, too!

After that, I stopped sharing any personal information with Tina, as did everyone else in the office. Andrea stopped listening to her, too. Without her busy bee pastime to rely on, Tina actually had to start working. She quit a month later!

In this scenario, Andrea, the already aggressive Queen Bee boss, was spurred on to further destruction by her Middle Bee employee, Tina. The former Afraid-to-Bee author was scared to speak up, but once she did (with her husband's encouragement), she discovered her own power.

Isabelle, a swim coach and the mother of two girls, recalls a situation in which her volunteerism was undermined by a malicious Middle Bee.

It's ironic. I was providing my services free of charge, because my girls were swimming on a community team that didn't have a lot of money. Since I'd worked as a coach before (for pay), I was more than qualified. Compared to my other jobs, this team was pretty unsophisticated, and the male coach didn't have a lot of experience, so he was clearly intimidated by my background. But the bigger problem was the mothers of swimmers and one woman in particular, who began to gossip about me to both the head coach and the parents association. When I was shut out from coaching after one season without even a thank-you, it really hurt.

Years later, another mother from the parents association told me it had been that one woman who had presented me in the most negative light possible. She told the coach I bad-mouthed his abilities behind his back, which wasn't true, and suggested the swimmers didn't like me! The mom who finally shared this information said she spoke up in my defense, because her kids had been on the team and liked me. It didn't matter. The gossipy mother had created such animosity in the coach and other parents that I became a pariah and was never even asked to help or work at swim meets.

The Swarm

Sometimes Middle Bees work in groups, just as worker bees do in nature. Marie, a professional middle-aged woman, describes a situation where a campaign against her was mounted by her female coworkers. A group of Middle Bees passed rumors among themselves, feeding select tidbits to the Queen Bee, who was Marie's direct supervisor.

I started experiencing marital problems and real instability with my husband and, to make a long story short, we separated and divorced. Because of the close relationship I had with one guy at work who became a confidant, those women made it their business as almost kind of a witch hunt to plant seeds about us having an affair. I know this is what they did. They made sure that this particular story got to my boss, and it was really damaging.

I am convinced that from the time I walked in, they formed a particular impression and probably waited for the moment until they had that opportunity to put some things together. It (RA) became more intensified once my marital status changed. What was particularly offensive was that it was other women in the human resources department. I have been in HR close to thirty years, and I take the profession very seriously. I expect a lot from my colleagues in human resources, and I just thought the women were absolutely so unfaithful to that profession.

Powerhouse

In reality, the Middle Bee may be the most influential RA role. Middle Bees have the opportunity to change the RA dynamic by swinging a situation in favor of either the bully or the victim. Their ability to control the social atmosphere of any group means Middle Bees often determine whether the outcome of an interaction is helpful or harmful. As such, they can be just as supportive as they can be destructive.

When a Middle Bee comes forward and intervenes to right a wrong involving another woman, she demonstrates the positive potential of in-betweeners. Luanne Thorndyke, a physician and administrator at a large university, shared her philosophy of looking for women who've been underappreciated or even ignored and trying to help them develop professionally. When asked if she ever experienced RA as an adolescent, Luanne recalled an incident in which she acted to help a friend who was being bullied. It was a situation common to adolescents, with a group of girls singling out another to be their victim and teasing her relentlessly. By intervening to befriend and defend the victim, a pattern was set that would persist into adulthood. "I hadn't thought about it, but I guess my inclination to take action rather than accept the situation got its roots back then," she concluded, after reviewing the details of her high school experience.

Whether you are a woman paralyzed by fear or driven by insecurity, your role as the middle bystander or intervener can be the beginning or the end of an RA dynamic. Which role do you choose?

CHAPTER 5

Blindsided, Backstabbed, and Bruised

The Afraid-to-Bee

*It got so bad I was afraid to say anything for fear
she would snap my head off.*

—A MOTHER NEW TO A PTA THAT HAS A QUEEN BEE PRESIDENT

W omen who are stuck in the Afraid-to-Bee role have most
often been the target of one bully or another, sometimes
since adolescence. Though most women have experienced isolated
incidents of being stung by gossip, exclusion, or manipulation,
their feelings of betrayal and insecurity pass and life goes on. For
others, the role of victim can become internalized after repeated
or intense assaults.

If you wonder about your own potential as an Afraid-to-Bee,
answer the following questions and see how many of the behaviors apply to you.

1. As a young girl, were you often the victim of other girls'
   aggression?

2. Do you fail to express how you're really feeling out of fear
   of the repercussions?

3. Are you likely to go along with what other women want
   you to do, even if you don't want to?

4. Is it hard for you to try out new behaviors because you
   worry what others will think or say?

5. Will you do almost anything to avoid conflict with other women?

6. Do strong women intimidate you?

7. Do you think your friends are all more assertive than you?

8. Have you stayed in an unhappy work situation or friendship because you are afraid to change?

9. Do you find yourself secretly furious or depressed over the way other women treat you?

10. Would other women who know you describe your friendship style as "too nice" or "too giving?"

Wounded Women

Being targeted from a young age can cause girls to automatically assume the role of victim, placing themselves at risk for receiving violence throughout their lives. The author of the following story shares her experience, which illustrates how deeply RA can wound—and for how long these hurts can last.

Not the Good Old Days

LISA LONDON

Since the first day of kindergarten, I can recall being taunted and teased by the neighborhood bullies as well as the nonbullies. The nonbullies were the girls who just felt that they wouldn't be accepted by befriending someone who was continually picked on. Their form of bullying often plagued me more than the kids who saw me as a human punching bag.

Growing up in Flushing, New York, as an overweight, shy, naive, Jewish girl with an unusual last name that was easily converted into something unpleasant was pretty tough. Some of the toughest kids were bused in from Jamaica, New York, to attend the local elementary school. I attended this school from kindergarten through sixth grade before going on to junior high school. Those seven years were some of the toughest of my life. When people ponder their youth, they reflect on all the wonderful memories and how they would give anything to turn back the clock. Not me.

I lived only half a block from the school, which often felt like a mile and a half. Almost daily, I'd have to plan my route of escape to avoid being roughed up. Which stairway should I take, which door should I exit, how fast could I run? I often lost focus on the academics because of my deep-rooted concerns of survival just to make it back home.

My parents wondered what I was doing to cause someone to want to hurt me. The truth is, all kids had to do was look at me, and then they would repeat: "You're dead after school." The words ring in my ears to this very day.

Once I got into junior high school, the trail still followed me. The physical abuse was reduced but not eliminated. The verbal abuse continued as strong as ever. Puberty entered and with that came even more ridicule. My self-esteem was reduced to that of a crumb. Even people who claimed to be my friends didn't support me; they simply sat back and watched the show as punches, kicks, and insults flew.

By the time I was set to go to high school, my parents decided it was time to move before my life faced serious consequences. They learned that I would be scheduled to attend Jamaica High School, which, back in the early seventies, was like frontline war combat. So we finally moved, something I had been begging to do for close to ten years.

Moving to New City, New York, I still battled self-esteem issues that affected my relationships with some friends, but for the most part, it was the beginning of reinventing myself. No one knew the kid from Queens or what I had (barely) lived through. I definitely had some kinks to iron out in the beginning, but it paved the way for a path of renewed hope. Three years after the move, we moved again to suburban New Jersey. I was in my junior year of high school and I can say that for the first time ever, I was able to shake my past, had genuine friends, and was just known to others as Lisa.

Several years passed, and when I graduated from college and began looking for work, I once again felt similar pangs to that of my youth. Job interviews and rejection both socially and professionally led me to believe that some of what I had heard growing up might actually be true, even though this was a new kind of rejection. When I eventually did find work, I was often suspicious of my peers speaking negatively about me. If I must say so myself, I was and still am an outstanding employee. I didn't realize it at the time and, of course, all my fears were unfounded, but still, they were there.

I've worked for domineering men and women who have occasionally strong-armed me and tried to use their power to reduce me (and countless other employees) to dirt. I'm embarrassed to admit that I've cried openly out of humiliation from these superiors, because once again, my self-esteem was struck down.

My relationships with men followed a similar path until I met my husband. I never trusted men and often felt they hated me, even if they said they loved me. Somehow I knew that the man I eventually married was sincere. His childhood experiences nearly paralleled mine, and I felt confident that he would never do to me what countless others had done to both of us.

As I worked my way up the professional ladder in advertising and sales, I eventually earned the respect of my peers and superiors. It took many years of negotiating emotions and authority with these groups until they accepted that I wouldn't let others push me around, no matter how high up they were. I was no longer afraid to tactfully state my professional opinions and often changed the course of things for the better. As a salesperson, I was in the "people business," which is humbling considering my rocky beginnings with people, but I developed the confidence to conduct a meeting and close sales without feelings of failure. Even if the sale didn't happen, I never blamed myself; in fact, I used it as a challenge and a goal.

I've recently switched careers to teaching preschool and kindergarten-age children. At our school and at the school my children attend, there is a zero-tolerance bullying policy, something I wish I had when I was growing up. I hope that through my efforts as a teacher, a mother, and an involved school parent, I can prevent children from having to live through the kind of childhood (which in turn, can follow through to adulthood) that I had.

Like Lisa, victimized women are afraid—afraid to speak up, afraid to remove themselves from unhealthy situations, in short, they are Afraid-to-Bees who are too frightened to allow their real potential to be realized. Unfortunately, abusive women with Queen Bee or Middle Bee tendencies seem to have a flare for finding and exploiting those whom they perceive to be weaker or more fearful than they are. Coercion, harassment, exclusion, and a host of other behaviors can keep Afraid-to-Bee women victimized and stuck in feelings of fear and failure, sometimes indefinitely.

Dianne Schwartz, author of *Whose Face Is in the Mirror?* describes how to change this behavior. While her perspective relates to domestic abuse, many of the points she makes are relevant for Afraid-to-Bees who have retreated into the role of victim after an onslaught of RA. Schwartz suggests that the most important first step a woman can take to break free of targeted aggression is recognizing it, as Lisa in the previous story did. The reality of the situation is that she is being hurt and abused by another. Coupled with this realization must come the desire to end victimization, which will require change. Once these two insights have been achieved, the former victim needs to identify the kind of person she now wants to be and set rules for behavior that allow her to maintain self-respect. The last step is reeducating others in how to treat her.

Sometimes, there is no opportunity for a careful and deliberate change to occur. Many women who fit the Afraid-to-Bee description break free of victimization not by deliberate choice, but when a crisis occurs, as happened in the following story. Forced to take action after a series of escalating abuses, the author found that the tragedy of losing her job freed her from a Queen Bee who was poisoning her life.

In the Write Place
CARLY KITE

I had been working as an editor and writer at a magazine for about two years when my immediate boss quit and left me with the majority of our department's responsibilities while upper management searched for a replacement. For six months I did the work of two people, and though I was recognized with a company award for a job well done, the editor in chief thought I was too young and inexperienced to be promoted. The magazine hired Mona, a middle-aged divorcée who had relocated to be closer to a man she had met in our area. I was determined not to be bitter toward Mona and hoped instead to learn from her editorial experience and guidance.

Despite my best effort to acquaint Mona with everything I knew about the job and step out of the way so that she could lead, I learned quickly that she had a hidden agenda. From the first day, she arrived late, left early, and was gone from the office for hours at a time. She also had a host of problems stemming from the personal relationship with the man for whom she had moved to be near; sometimes she didn't come to work at all, and because I knew what to do in her absence, the job got done. Mona always appeared friendly to me on the surface, but as I was the only one who truly knew her work ethic, it became clear that she intended to make me quit.

In meetings between the two of us, she repeatedly crushed my enthusiasm and ideas with sarcastic comments such as, "Aren't you ambitious?" and "Maybe you're not ready to handle that quite yet." Then she began attacking me personally on a daily basis, noting that I looked tired or sick or upset and asking time and again, "What's wrong?" I was neither tired nor sick and despite my assurance that I was fine, she would make a puppy dog face and shake her head in disbelief. At staff celebrations for birthdays or holidays, Mona would point out that I wasn't eating any cake and then utter in a nasty tone, "You're so good. What willpower you have." (She knew that I was training to run a marathon and trying to lose weight in the process.) Other times she would make catty comments about my body type saying, "You're not built to be a runner because you carry all your weight in your legs. You should really stick to biking."

As I became increasingly frustrated with her apathy toward the job and her negativity toward me, I tried to avoid her whenever possible. She must have sensed as much, because one day she took me out to lunch and asked me why I didn't want to be her friend. She then requested that I be more open with her by sharing my personal life. Knowing that she was horribly insecure and manipulative and that anything I told her most likely would be twisted and used against me, I responded that I didn't feel comfortable discussing my life outside of work due to our professional relationship.

Over time, Mona began hiring her friends as freelance writers, even though she knew I wanted the assignments and would offer a cheaper alternative. Mona was phasing me out of my own job and I was powerless to stop it. I also am quite sure, though I have no proof, that she misrepresented my performance to the editor in chief. Eventually, the magazine was forced to make cuts to its editorial staff, and though I had worked there longer, had never had a negative performance evaluation, and maintained a far better relationship with the rest of the staff, I was laid off. Immediately after I learned the news of my layoff, Mona ran up to me and asked, "What are you going to do? The job market is so bad. Do you have a plan?" I held my tongue and left that office forever a few days later. Initially, I had an extremely hard time dealing with the injustice of all that occurred, but in retrospect, freedom from Mona's toxic personality is the greatest gift I could have received.

Each of these Afraid-to-Bees validate that the victim role does not need to continue in adulthood, no matter how deeply ingrained the behavior is. Afraid-to-Bees can learn that underneath, the fear they feel is not so different from the insecurity that leads Queen Bees to lash out with aggression in preemptive attempts to prevent others from hurting them. For both types, and Middle Bees as well, an inner fear or sense of threat that leads to unhealthy outward behaviors is often built on false information. Understanding and believing this is an important step for victims who need to change their behavior from passive to powerful.

Caught by Surprise

As shown in the following story, when a woman is devious and intent on sabotage, you can be blindsided into the victim role. Unsure of how to respond in a new job, the author of the following story found herself a "situational victim."

Leaving Doris and Frank
TERRY L. HEFFELFINGER

The longest fifteen months of my life were working with Doris, a sixtyish, white-haired woman, and our boss, Frank. It became my life's emotional watershed, where with help, I summoned the courage to stand up to a bully and got out.

I was single, twenty-five years old, and had just left a great secretarial job. I had been the only woman in a large group of men who treated me with kindness and respect. My job was being phased out, so I looked for a transfer within the company. The interview for the new job had gone well, but I had not interviewed with Frank.

The first day on the job was full of Frank yelling, using abusive language, and then coming back from lunch drunk. I called my old boss to try to get my job back. He said it wouldn't be in my best interest and then hung up.

Doris was right there when I got off the phone. She smiled as if she had found my on-off switch. To make my work life miserable, she began telling Frank about every mistake I made.

One Friday before a long holiday weekend, Frank called me into his office after Doris had pointed out a typo to him. I said politely that the day before I had found an error that would have overpaid a contractor by $100,000.

Frank said convincingly, "Damn it, I'm tired of your mistakes! When you come in here on Tuesday morning, I'm going to blow your head off with an Uzi machine gun."

The comment launched a weekend-long panic attack. I wanted to die rather than go back to work. I called a crisis hotline and sought help. I was referred to a therapist, who helped me to find the courage to make a plan to get out of there.

Doris controlled my coming and going. She created a sign in/out sheet, allegedly for the entire office. The men, including Frank, ignored it, but I was not allowed to even go to the bathroom or the copier without signing in and out. She had a lock put on the copier room door, and I had to ask for a key from her every time I needed to make copies.

Before she would give me the key, Doris demanded to know what I was going to copy; then she would write my name on a slip of paper along with the reason for the copy. She kept the record in her drawer.

Often when Doris returned from the copier, she would smirk and put a copy of a recipe on my desk. If I did the same, she would report me to Frank.

When Doris knew she had overstepped her boundaries, she tried to be nice. Too nice. She would give me things in her lunch like juice boxes. I would say no thanks, but she insisted I have them and harangued me until I took them. I angrily sipped away.

Doris kept her part of the work process private, believing that it kept her job secure. When she would take a day off, everything would stop because no one knew where Doris kept her logs or her keys.

When we got a new printer, Doris thought letters on official letterhead could not be printed on it. I secretly worked at it until I got it right and then showed her the letter I had printed, perfectly aligned with the letterhead. Doris was angry and I was delighted. The confidence I got from that letter spurred me on to other acts of civil disobedience.

When Frank put up a poster in his office of a bare-breasted woman, I protested. Frank said it was none of my damn business, and he could do whatever he wanted in his office. Doris asked me if I was having an affair with Frank. I ignored her.

Soon after, I found out that employees could use a half hour from their lunch periods to apply for new jobs. I wrote out my application at home, and then every day for a week, I typed it. I applied for a promotion to another secretarial job.

I had an interview within a month. Two managers were interviewing for two jobs, so I had my pick of whom to work for. I chose my boss based on his personality and distance from my current office.

I went back to the office and gave my two-weeks' notice. Frank said he didn't know who the hell would hire me. Doris laughed. I smiled back and then asked Doris for the keys to the copier. I locked myself in the room and jumped up and down for joy. In two weeks, this nightmare would be over.

Although she didn't initially know how to respond, this Afraid-to-Bee finally discovered a way to take back the power that the Middle Bee, Doris, had temporarily stolen from her.

At-Risk Victims

Aggression seems to begin when one woman feels threatened by another. For example, physically attractive women are often singled out for resentment the minute they walk into a room. In her article "Beautiful Losers," Heather Mallick, a reporter for the *Toronto Sun*, wrote about the perils of being a beautiful woman, commenting that no one has much sympathy for a person who claims to be handicapped by her looks. The book *The Power of Beauty* by Nancy Friday cites studies that show beautiful women receive higher salaries and other benefits because of their appearance, thereby positioning them for resentment from other women. It is harder to be an attractive woman than an attractive man: studies show women are more hostile toward glamorous individuals from their same sex than men are.

Many women have written about situations in which an attractive female gets treated aggressively (that is, "stung") solely on the basis of her looks and then responds with either aggressive or passive behavior. Beautiful women admit they often choose to befriend other beautiful women for this reason.

Jess, a college student, told me, "Attractive girls tend to associate only with other attractive girls for the most part, and they joke about those who are perceived as less attractive. Ethnic groups do the same thing. They only associate with people of the same ethnic background (that is, blacks stay with blacks, whites stay with whites)."

Another source of targeting for women is body size. Those who are thinner often receive both praise and putdowns for their physique, regardless of whether they come by their build through genetics or the gym. In a newsletter article about eating disorders, one college coed commented that it wasn't the catcalls and comments of guys that made her self-conscious about her body, it was the calculating looks of women who "sized her up."

Even in ways that are almost comical, women can use appearance to put another woman down, as the following story shows.

Toe to Toe

SHERILYN LEE

I didn't think it was such a big deal. If I got to it, I got to it. If I didn't, I didn't. Besides, I agonize over other things. For example, my face is peeled and waxed at three-week intervals. I apply lip liner, because lipstick alone isn't enough. As an engineer, I wear clean, matching clothes that were purchased after I graduated from college. I watch how much and what I eat. My hair stylist selects my cut and color, because the style I want isn't always the one I can wear well. I floss. But none of my conscientious self-care mattered when two women from my company's accounting department studied my feet.

"I just can't go out wearing open-toed shoes without painted toenails," said the one from accounts receivable to the other from accounts payable.

They grinned at each other. Their faceless, uniformed army of perfectly painted toenails outnumbered me two to one, and I was ambushed.

Up to this point in my life, the only attention my size six-and-a-half feet ever received was preceded by the exclamation, "Look how tiny your feet are!" Now I couldn't even look at my naked feet without feeling differently about them.

I admit my toenails do look nicer when I paint them, but this requires planning and effort. My painted toes don't look just right until I put lotion on them, which leads to selecting the right shoes, which affects my clothes and jewelry choices. Toenail management begins innocently but quickly becomes oppressive.

My boss walked into my office as I mumbled something unprofessional and uncharitable about the company's pedicure jury. I responded to his puzzled look by unleashing the details of my encounter with the accounting department.

He shrugged his shoulders. "My wife does hers while watching Oprah."

She does. I could. But, above all, he doesn't ever have to.

As Sherilyn shows, even the tiniest detail of a woman's appearance can set her apart from her peers and create the potential for targeting. Basically, any woman who challenges the status quo may become at risk for victimization. Like her beautiful counterpart, she stands out because she is different and therefore a potential threat. Consider Marissa's experience: "When we moved, my husband's boss suggested we buy a house in an old, established community where several of his coworkers already lived. The week we arrived, a party was held to greet us, and I thought the other women, most of whom were stay-at-home moms like me, would become a wonderful group of new friends," Marissa confided.

Unfortunately, Marissa soon found herself trying in every way she could think of to break into a clique of women who were polite but never accepted her invitations to drop by for coffee or go for a walk with their children. While Marissa's husband had no trouble assimilating into the lunch and after-work crowd of the women's spouses, at home, Marissa remained an outsider with the wives. "They wouldn't even include me in their carpool," she recalls bitterly, going on to describe the family's eventual move to another neighborhood at her instigation.

Marissa found herself excluded and perhaps targeted, forced into a classic Afraid-to-Bee situation in which she worried that her every word and gesture might further alienate her from the group.

One of the most striking "newcomer" situations I know of occurred at a college where I taught. Debra, a bright, cheerful nurse practitioner, was hired to fill an administrative position that offered exciting opportunities. While I rarely think of professional colleagues as lovely, that's the word that describes Debra. All of my coworkers liked her from the start—everyone, that is, but Andrea, who had wanted Debra's position, even though her qualifications weren't appropriate.

Just as our faculty responded to Debra's arrival with warmth, many of us had learned to avoid Andrea. Over the years, we put distance between her and us because of her penchant for causing trouble, with the help of another faculty member, Lydia. Lydia was a master at spreading rumors and would often initiate a conversation for the purpose of gaining information she could then twist into gossip and share with Andrea. While Middle Bee Lydia planted seeds of hostility, Andrea went further, spending hours in our dean's office shredding the reputation of her latest victim.

Debra's new job made her Andrea's supervisor, forcing her into constant contact with a woman whose personality can only be described as toxic, unpredictable, and devious. Over the first year of her employment, Debra deteriorated from an articulate, happy teacher to a bitter, harried woman. It happened gradually, but by the end of twelve months, Andrea's continual manipulation and undermining (with Lydia's help) proved too much for even Debra's once-sunny personality. Convinced that both students and faculty had no confidence in her, she requested to switch out of her administrative position to full-time teaching. Not surprisingly, Andrea got Debra's job, and with their roles reversed, the aggression became worse.

Andrea didn't physically abuse Debra. She didn't rob her or cause her to lose her job, but in hundreds of small ways she did all those things by telling secretaries to do Debra's work last, discrediting Debra to students, and commissioning her office for someone else. In face-to-face interactions, Andrea was supersweet to Debra; behind her back she was as malevolent as a Queen Bee in full attack mode.

Debra's health and marriage began to suffer. She lost so much confidence in her abilities she ended up resigning and moving to another state. And Andrea? She continued on, destroying more careers and driving other women away. Lydia, her Middle Bee helper who worked from behind the scenes, also remained unscathed. Those of us who watched were victims like Debra. We tried to help, but found our efforts futile and our own reputations targeted. Now that I understand RA and its devastating consequences, I wish I had tried to do more to support Debra.

The situation has striking parallels to stories I've heard from adolescent girls, with one major difference: while teenagers have an entire future to explore more positive situations and learn to empower themselves, Debra was on the downslope of her career. Her life was permanently changed by Andrea, and she suffered financially, emotionally, physically, and professionally. As with many Afraid-to-Bees, the consequences of a Queen Bee attack derailed her completely. Years later, I still think of Debra and hope that wherever she is, the trauma of the abuse she received from Andrea has somehow receded. I know it will take me and the others who witnessed it a long time to forget.

CHAPTER 6

Weapons of Choice

You know the expression "claw her eyes out?" I wanted to.

—A DIVORCÉE WHO DISCOVERED HER HUSBAND'S
MISTRESS WAS A CLOSE FRIEND

Adolescent girls use relationships as a way to aggress, with words and behavior the weapons they wield against one another. Increasingly, RA in girls is escalating to the point of physical violence as extreme as shootings. In adult women, aggression plays out in relational ways, too, relying on nonphysical behaviors guaranteed to hurt in ways that leave neither an outward bruise or visible wound. With age, however, the RA tactics employed by Queen Bees and Middle Bees tend to become more sophisticated and are refined to what one woman described as an "art form."

Vicki, a mom from an affluent community, says, "Women here are very skilled at what I call 'face.' I think that may actually be a Japanese term, but as I'm using it, I mean putting on one expression for the world to see, but secretly letting the mask off with some other women. I go to school to pick up my kids and see lots of 'faces,' meaning moms who look like they're friendly and well-adjusted. Then I interact with them one-on-one, and the real person comes out. They're all threatened by each other, regarding who has what and whose kids have accomplished the most. It's not pretty."

Kendra, a businesswoman, remarks on how women respond when a colleague rises to a position of power: "I think a lot of women speak out of both sides of their mouths. On the one hand, there is a cry for female leadership, because there is none. But when a woman is in that leadership role and has to come across as a strong woman, other women can be incredibly catty. If you remove yourself from those kinds of alliances, you are viewed in a particular way: others are not going to associate with you, they don't like you, and so on. I think women revert to that cattiness because they don't view it as a woman doing her job, and they take her actions personally. If it was a man they wouldn't respond in the same way."

Mary, another woman familiar with the study of RA, observed: "Adult women are less likely to do these things openly to friends, or maybe adult friends simply won't tolerate such behavior. At the same time, the lines are less clear for grown women. Girls think of relationships as 'either-or,' but as adults there still can be elements of rivalry and low-level RA, even among women who are close and get along."

For some women, competition may be the underlying theme in any relationship, friendly or not. In the book *Catfight!* author Leora Tanenbaum suggests that the majority of conflicts among women comes from a need to be better than one's peers, no matter what the venue. When a woman perceives the need to compete, Tanenbaum believes she will respond aggressively.

The following story demonstrates just how aggressive women can become, even when the stakes are small, and even when the women appear to be, at least superficially, friends. The dynamic described by Chris can become such an ingrained interaction pattern that both parties fail to recognize it for what it is.

Competitive Camaraderie
CHRIS KING

Every Sunday morning at nine o'clock, T and I meet in the Starbucks parking lot. T is Theresa; we have been T and C for about ten years now. I beat her there by a few minutes and gloat because I scored the primo parking spot. Instantly, I wince, because I hate to do that and catch myself doing it nevertheless. Years of competing with Theresa are beginning to bore me.

Theresa arrives, her hair emerging first from her white Jaguar. She is all about big hair; when that phrase was coined, she was the model. She's a little person, much shorter than me, and teensy despite the fact that she obsesses about her weight and size. It's nearly criminal that we whine equally about our weight problems. She is always the one whom men look at when we're together; she's simply got that look. Me, I'm one of those people who rarely get remembered for my looks.

We meet for our walk along the lake. We do three miles round-trip every weekend while we talk, and finish with coffee and scones back at Starbucks. This morning, I don't even get a hello; she's got something to battle about.

"Did you climb Mt. Si yesterday?" she asks.

"Yes, Jim and I did. It was unbelievably difficult. I can barely walk today," I answer, just waiting to bask in my anticipated glory. After all, Mt. Si is the mother of all local hikes; it's what you strive for once you're in shape.

"How far was it?"

"Eight miles round-trip, four up to the summit."

Before I could say anything else, she hoots with laughter. "Ha, I went farther than you. Our hike was nine miles! Patty and I did Tiger Mountain; we didn't realize how steep and long it was. It was really a hard workout; we could barely carry on a conversation." She was blathering on.

I was still back at the "Ha, I went farther than you" comment. Now, why that bothered me so much was unclear; after all, isn't this the juice of our relationship? Isn't competition what we're often about, much as I dislike that?

I become aware that I'd stopped listening, but she went on talking about her hiking feat. I hear "nya nya nya 2,000-foot elevation . . . nya nya . . . so tired, nya summit nya."

What I see now is not my big-haired, competitive friend, but a little girl cowering in front of her judgmental mother, saying, "Look, Momma, here's my A paper . . . no, I guess somebody got an A+, I know you were an A+ student. And yes, I gained two pounds since I saw you last. Please Momma, I'm a good girl, aren't I? You love me, don't you, Momma?"

I'm overwhelmed with sorrow. Just then T says, "So what was your elevation gain?"

"Thirty-one hundred feet in four miles."

She mumbles "oh" in a clearly defeated tone. I had her finally, but the glory was moot.

When a "victory" occurs at the expense of another woman's feelings, even the fiercest female competitor feels something less than triumph. Unlike men, who tend to strive for a goal single-mindedly, women frequently define success as approval and acceptance as well as achievement.

The Sharpest Sting

In nature, the Queen Bee never loses her stinger. She can use it over and over again and does, usually to battle another candidate for Queen Bee to the death. As adults, women can be equally vicious: undermining, manipulating, backstabbing, blindsiding, betraying, excluding, gossiping, teasing in a hurtful way and then pretending to be joking, targeting another woman's children, humiliating, harassing, and misrepresenting. These are the most common weapons found in the RA stockpiles of grown women, but as the following post from "govworkr" to my message board suggests, cliques survive into adulthood, too.

> My experience centers on a clique of mid-management women in a local agency and the havoc they raise, using the powers of their office to alter documents and spread rumors, all aimed at taking down those who oppose them and instilling fear in their subordinates. I walk a fine line between performing my duties and maintaining my employment at this agency. As agents of the government, the women are protected and work as a bunch of rogue agents with supervisors who absently and openly grant deference to the decisions of the rogues, terming them the professionals and experts. This occurs despite the total disregard for information and opinion offered by the medical and psychological communities who challenge the actual opinions and decisions.
>
> I am a master's-level educator in the triple fields related to my job with thirty years of experience. I've received several awards for my work. For the past three years, I have been tackling perhaps the most convoluted odyssey of my experience— an odyssey at the hands of these select, two-faced female aggressors utilizing their powers over the office to enhance their relational aggressive characteristics. At the onset of this

latest journey, I was challenged with questions of why these women would do that if they didn't really believe it. I suggested that they were women who never really outgrew that group of girls we all recognize from junior high.

In the book *In the Company of Women*, authors Pat Heim and Susan Murphy detail behaviors that women use in the workplace to undermine other behaviors, not so different from the ones listed in the prior story. Gossip, breaking confidences, put-downs, sabotage, and withholding friendship are the keys to aggressing against coworkers.

Mariah, a middle-aged white-collar woman who relocated to take an exciting new job, experienced these behaviors, which were targeted at her by her female coworkers: "I actually had always had very strong female networks, and it was very difficult for me when I came to the company, because from the minute I arrived it was very, very clear that 'you are from the outside; we don't like outsiders.' I was excluded, talked about, and treated rudely. At the time, they really hadn't brought people in from the outside and when they did, it was because they weren't able to get whatever technical expertise they needed from inside. I quickly understood why."

A Continuum of Aggression

The following story describes so many typical RA behaviors (gossip, exclusion, misrepresenting, intimidation, undermining, backstabbing, manipulating, and ridicule disguised as humor) that if you fail to read carefully, you might assume it was about adolescents.

Bully Girl

LINDA JORDAN TUCKER

Kate grabbed my wrist, pulled me aside, and hissed, "You won't believe what just happened between that horrible Gail and me!" Eyes flashing with anger, she spilled the tale of her altercation with Gail, and said to me decisively, "We don't like her anymore, okay?"

I was stunned and speechless. Were we on the playground at recess? No. In spite of the fourth grade sound of her proclamation, we weren't kids at all. Kate and I were colleagues, working in academe as adult women. The childishness of her words made me realize that Kate was a bully, and suddenly my own uneven relationship with her came into focus.

Anyone meeting Kate for the first time would find her attractive, charming, and witty. Even a brief acquaintance would reveal, however, that her humor is sharply mocking and derisive, and everything about you is fair game to her: your haircut, clothes, office and home decor, friends. As for her own friends, unlike people who want all their pals to know one another, Kate does not like to share. This was made painfully evident to me when I first came to work at our university.

Aware that I was newly hired, Kate, whom I had met in graduate school, offered to show me around campus and introduce me to my new colleagues. As soon as we arrived at a meeting, she spotted an old friend and hurried to his side. As I made my way to them, she stood on tiptoe, whispered in his ear, threw back her head, and laughed loudly. Standing there un-introduced, I had a flashback: the faculty meeting had suddenly become the school yard playground of my youth, where the easiest way to torment a child was to whisper to another in her presence.

Throughout that day, Kate continued to plunge into animated conversations as soon as we encountered her colleagues. She rarely introduced me and even turned her back to me so she stood between me and anyone she talked to. Quickly taking control of the flow of a conversation, she steered it to topics I had no part of.

Kate's body language could not have been clearer: these people "belonged" to her, and she had no intention of sharing them with me. Despite her offer to acquaint me with coworkers and campus life, it was evident she wanted to exclude me at every opportunity.

In spite of her, I settled into life at the university. I loved my job; my other colleagues were welcoming, and my students responded well to my teaching. The more successful I became in my new role, however, the cooler and more distant Kate grew. Eventually she hardly spoke to me. She continued to employ the tricks of the school yard bully: she made nasty comments about me to others and had parties but did not invite me. I was oblivious to her social plans, however, so she was forced to send one of her friends to inform me that I had been excluded! Once again the bully's target, I was reminded of grade-school tactics used to wound and embarrass.

I think Kate must have been a bully as a child, as well—not a hair-pulling, give-me-your-lunch-money kind of bully, but a less obvious, more insidious kind. She was the girl who asserted her power by involving others in her quarrels so that her enemies were shunned by an entire group; the girl who ridiculed other girls' physical appearances, the girl who whispered nasty things behind her hand and made sure that the subject of her gossip was aware of the whisper; the girl who used social invitations as a weapon. Her bullying techniques continue to be effective and the number of her victims has grown. Most don't know what has hit them, and the rest wouldn't expect such behavior from an attractive professional woman. And that is this bully's best disguise.

By adulthood, women who internalized RA behaviors in the teen years have perfected their ability to aggress with a smile. Victims of such sweet hostility may feel as if they have been magically transported back to middle school, where such behaviors were commonplace and even tolerated. In adulthood, however, women such as Kate miss a multitude of opportunities that might afford them true friendships.

Guess What I Just Heard!

In the *Psychology Today* article "Evolved to Chat: The New Word on Gossip," Professor Nigel Nicholson describes how gossip can actually be beneficial by forging connections between people and even building alliances. There is a difference, however, between sharing information and stories and deliberately twisting content for hurtful purposes. In a study on communication mentioned in the article, both genders were found to be more likely to encourage than discourage initiation of gossip, but women used negative gossip more than men. Nicholson warns against negative gossip, the practice of passing on malicious content from a rumormonger who pretends to be concerned about the gossiped-about but absent party.

A better rule of thumb is to think before you talk and determine whether another woman would be hurt by what you say. If you don't know whether the information you're about to pass on is true, be careful of what you repeat. As Nicholson warns, such sharing can often backfire on those involved, as happened in the following story.

My Best Friend and Secret Enemy

Patricia Duff

Gossip isn't meant to be exposed, especially if you are the one being gossiped about. When it happened to me, I felt violated and uncertain of how to handle the situation. I had never been the victim of gossip before, at least not to my knowledge, and suddenly it felt like I was thrust back into seventh grade, only now I was no longer the happy-go-lucky fourteen-year-old everyone loved and admired. I knew what if felt like to be the girl who suffered the arrows of bitter words that stung her from behind the backs of hands.

Our daughters became fast friends at age three, sharing play dates frequently, which allowed Jen and I to become more than acquaintances. We got to know each other over many cups of tea, discussing good novels, and even going to see some bad theater together, which is always a bonding experience. I realized she was a person who shared things: the more I saw of her the more I noticed her penchant for sharing not-so-nice-things about others.

I discussed it with my husband, and he said I should just stop seeing Jen, but our girls were best friends. I thought maybe I could steer our conversations away from gossip and become a positive influence. I knew it had something to do with her insecurities, and that she was probably just feeling badly about herself.

Then Jen began to subtly direct her hostility toward me. I was baffled and pondered whether or not to challenge inferences she made about my parenting style or my children's behavior.

Jen became sick with breast cancer and, almost immediately after chemotherapy, injured herself in a fall while vacationing.

Her sickness aroused my sympathy, and I let certain hostile remarks that seemed random and unfounded hover and fade, believing she needed to take out her aggression on someone who seemed to have no problems.

But my annoyance turned into ire when I learned that she had been speaking badly of me to other mothers at the school. I had noticed certain people not meeting my eye on occasion in an obvious effort to avoid speaking to me, but finding out that Jen had said untrue things about me was more than I could stand. I wrote her a letter and said all the things I wanted to say to her. I was direct without being hostile. I was sincere when I showed concern that our children might suffer the loss of a friend. I was honest about being hurt. And I was tough when I told her to stop using me as fodder for her conversations. It felt good to write it, and I know I did the right thing.

Jen called me almost immediately after she received the letter. We both agreed that we should meet and have a conversation. I'm hoping it goes well and that something is resolved, and although I have forgiven her on some level, I don't think I will ever be able to completely trust her again. That, I believe, is a great loss to her.

Exchanging information about someone in a factual way, clarifying details on an incident or person, and sharing stories in the manner of the time-honored tradition of storytelling do not fall into the category of gossip. These types of conversations aren't started to harm or discredit another woman; however, rumors, campaigns, innuendos, and betraying confidences are. Questions you can ask to determine if gossip is malicious include:

- Would I want this said about me?
- Is the only reason for saying this to put down another?
- Does it feel wrong in my gut when I say it?
- Does it escalate a negative story about someone else?

Not Quite Fistfights

As with our adolescent counterparts, RA can be as subtle as the passing put-down, more overt like the biting barb, or an all-out campaign to destroy another woman. Although physical intimidation is rare, some women may resort to this behavior or the implied threat of it as demonstrated in the following stories.

In My Space
KATHYLYNN LaPAN

At a young age, I became a medical secretary at my hometown hospital. Marie, an older woman who had worked at the hospital for twenty-five years, was to orient me.

The problem started when, shortly after my arrival, the hospital implemented a new patient ordering system based on an Intranet. I had computer experience; Marie did not.

I turned out to have a great aptitude for the job and did really well, which I believe caused Marie to be jealous, particularly because I replaced her on the evening shift when she switched to days. The quality of Marie's work began slipping. As the secretary on duty after her, I couldn't help noticing, because I had to finish what she left undone.

I began receiving complaints from our floor supervisor. She said I dressed "slutty" and wore too much makeup, although I did not wear any makeup or perfume. Marie was known for her thick blue eye shadow and heavy scents. One of the floor nurses, hearing the complaint, pointed this out, suggesting perhaps the complaint was about Marie, and that's when things got really bad.

First came notes calling me stupid and left in patient charts for me to find. Then there were complaints to our floor supervisor saying I'd left work undone. This continued until a complaint came in that I'd left work all weekend, on a weekend I'd had off! There were nasty notes in disguised handwriting on my locker, and when I was floated to other floors, I'd find the nurses wary of me and seeming surprised when I was polite and efficient.

I didn't connect all this until one night on my regular floor when our aide asked me why I'd attacked Marie in the parking lot. Shocked, I asked where she'd heard that. "Oh," she said, "everyone knows it was you. That's why Marie's out of work."

Marie was actually out for surgery. I went to the supervisor and told her everything that had happened, but since Marie was on sick leave, she decided to ignore it and see what happened when she came back.

Marie returned with a vengeance. At this same time I became pregnant, and Marie told everyone in the hospital that I didn't know who the father was. (I did.) She also told our supervisor that I said I didn't have to do anything right because I was pregnant, and that I'd threatened to beat her and our floor aide up in the parking lot.

Finally, I came to work early to confront Marie face-to-face. I cornered her in the break room and asked her what I had done to deserve this treatment, especially because when I had started, we'd been on the way to becoming friends.

"I've been here longer than you've been alive, you little bitch," she spat. "Don't tell me how to do my job! I am the lead secretary and that's it!" There was no such position as lead secretary at our hospital, but if there had been, I would have been happy to let her have it.

Shortly after this confrontation, I left work on maternity leave and didn't return to the hospital. Friends of mine who work there tell me that Marie is still talking about me more than three years later. Though things never got physical, there was more than one occasion when I was frightened for my safety. Marie was the epitome of a school yard bully grown up.

Lest it appear that professional women don't engage in physically intimidating behaviors, consider what Barb, a physician, tells about an incident she experienced in medical school.

It was a busy day, and I had worked about thirty-six hours straight. I had to go to a conference at 5 P.M. It was about 3 P.M. when I was thrown into using the laparoscopic camera for the first time. There were all women in the room, and not one gave me the ground rules of how to use the equipment, withholding even the simplest thing such as the fact that all the images on the screen were reversed.

"Pull that camera in," the other physician, a female surgeon, snapped at me when I hesitated.

I kept looking at the clock every minute, telling myself I was not going to cry. My hands were shaking, and I kept messing up. When it was over, I told the surgeon that I had to go to a conference.

"Where the hell do you think you're going?" She physically grabbed me; she was six feet, much taller than me. Luckily, she was called out of the room just then, and I burst into tears.

Later I had to walk around and do rounds with her. She was very sweet to the patients, but she treated male residents just as badly. She was fairly good to the nurses, but they catered to her. I think she trained to be them that way.

Ladies, Choose Your Weapon

While the battleground shifts from school hallways to coffee rooms and carpools, aggression among women in adulthood still uses relationships rather than fists to deliver blows. Usually, adolescents have a fairly limited repertoire of cruel behaviors and reasons for targeting others (mostly physical attributes, clothing, or relationships with boys). In contrast, grown women can be almost professional in their aggression, humiliating peers in front of superiors, attacking across multiple domains, and ferreting out and exploiting another's deepest vulnerabilities. In the presence of a vicious adult Queen Bee, it may be exclusion from "the hive" and a painful sting when you least expect it—at work, at home, or at play.

PART TWO

Our Own Worst Enemies

Aggression at Home, at Work, and at Play

Take me down a notch, attack me
with words, with rumors which are
words made sharper, cutting, untrue.
I think of that commercial
"Don't hate me because I'm beautiful."
Thick, shiny, lustrous hair-lips-face.
That isn't me. But I want to say
"Don't hate me because I'm talented"
or "Don't hate me because I'm smart."
Because you do, I can see it.
I can feel it—hear it—taste it.

ALIZA SHERMAN, "TAKE ME DOWN"

CHAPTER 7

Women at Work

So then it was like the same old same old, here we
go again, women eating their young.

—A WOMAN IN HER EARLY TWENTIES WHO
RECENTLY LEFT A JOB DUE TO RA

A s the number of women pursuing professional careers increases, there is bound to be some level of competition among them in the workplace, just as there is for men. The phenomenon of "bully bosses" seems to apply to both sexes, but some believe women take aggression to new extremes in attempts to appear as tough as their male counterparts. Women also are unique in their longing to be liked by their coworkers, whether they are subordinate or not.

"I found myself talking about a coworker who didn't really like me to my husband, and then realized that never in ten years of marriage had he worried a bit about how his coworkers feel about him!" mused one young woman. When she surveyed her female colleagues, she found they, too, had said or heard similar things— but never from a man.

Going It Alone

Although a bit of good-natured rivalry has the potential to inspire, it can poison the workplace environment for women. Perhaps we are only beginning to learn the concepts of networking and teamwork long understood by men. For every story printed here, I received two more suggesting that the workplace brings out the worst of RA tendencies. Despite our inherent orientation toward connections, many women have yet to master and use the power generated by a group of like-minded individuals striving for a common goal.

As one male administrator observed, "Women destroy each other. They haven't learned the win-win concept. For them, it's 'I win, you lose' or vice versa."

Give Me Shelter

Ironically, some organizations that would seem most dedicated to promoting positive relationships among women are the very ones where RA runs rampant. After many women involved in female-oriented or all-female professions and even feminist organizations contacted me, I decided this was an important issue to address. There was a special kind of betrayal experienced when an all-female environment that women thought would be more supportive and nurturing than one dominated by men turned out to be less so.

Each author had her own thoughts on why hurtful behaviors are almost epidemic in workplaces with a feminist philosophy, and some offered helpful strategies for change.

And Justice for All
LAURA HOLDEN

As somebody who is currently employed by a feminist social justice organization, I am sad to say that I have seen much bullying and relational aggression between adult women in my office and within the women's movement in general. Even Capitol Hill, where aggressiveness and bullying are usually the only means to achieve your desired outcomes, was tame compared to this.

Needless to say, I was completely shocked when I was indoctrinated into the women's community and discovered that behind the facade of wanting to help women, the women employed to improve women's lives actually treat each other and their subordinates like dirt. I find it to be an extremely deceitful and hypocritical community, run almost entirely by females who redefine narcissism. The women I interact with in the feminist movement are employed by organizations that say they exist to "make the world a better place" for women, yet in reality, they make the world a living hell for women they interact with. Simply put, it is unacceptable for men to oppress women, but it is perfectly acceptable, even expected, for women to oppress other women.

The women I work with thrive on their positions of power, humiliating and degrading the women who work for them and with them. They thrive on terrorizing women and beating them into submission. They treat other women in a way that they would never tolerate from a man, and, what is worse, they fail to realize the hypocrisy of the situation. The female president has seen to it that the few men employed here are treated with far more respect and are given far more responsibility than all of the women—except for herself.

I have my theories on why this is the case. Having carefully observed my boss, who is approaching sixty and has been active in the women's rights community since the early 1970s, it is obvious that she is insecure. She feels threatened by other women and men. She is fearful of not being respected and fearful of being viewed as anything other than omnipotent. As a result, she overcompensates for her insecurities by inflicting her wrath on her staff, intimidating us and questioning our intelligence and capabilities, which in turn severely diminishes our self-esteem. Our diminished, or in some cases nonexistent, self-esteem makes us self-conscious and leads us not to question her or defend ourselves when she launches personal attacks. She rules by fear, demanding respect instead of earning it, and terminates staff members who challenge her authority and refuse to fall victim to her oppressive mode of operation.

I also think that my employer is insanely jealous of women on staff who are happy and fulfilled with their personal lives, especially women with families and/or many close friendships. My employer is single, childless, and friendless. She has no close relationships with anyone, no family and no friends, and she has nothing of meaning in her life except for her job. I have gotten past the anger, because finally I understand that she truly is an insecure, lonely, bitter woman who tries to cover up for those feelings by inflating her self-esteem and importance. Now I feel nothing but pity for her and will always use her as an example of the type of person I never want to become.

If anybody tells you that bullying and relational aggression do not exist among adult women, they're either lying or they are extremely unobservant. I witness it every day in an atmosphere where there should be no room for such behavior.

The "woman hurting woman" message of this story makes one wonder if grown up mean girls gravitate to all-female organizations. The author of the following piece remarked on the irony of having published an academic article on this same topic in India.

Fractured
NEEMA CAUGHRAN, PH.D.

When I was the executive director of a women's commission, the public funding was decreasing and we were forced to begin talks of reorganization and layoffs. One employee, Marie, had previously been hired by her mother-in-law, Lynn, who had been the chair of the commission. Lynn led the commission in a time of terrible controversy, and I had since defended her name on more than one occasion. Yet, when the possibility of being laid off arose, Marie came to a meeting while I was out of town, accused me of embezzling funds, and handed out copies of my pay stubs. This was illegal, so we did indeed have to let Marie go. In truth, I had not paid myself anything for several months so that other employees, including Marie, could be paid. Still, she insisted I had been overpaid and implied I had taken a large sum of money, which was accounted for in the minutes of previous meetings that were public record. Marie and Lynn took their story to the city council members and county board of supervisors. The city auditor found no evidence of any wrongdoing, but once any accusation is made, people believe it and the commission's stature in the community was affected. The aftershock went on for months, and Marie is now suing the commission and me, one year later. Initially I was angry, hurt, and dumbfounded, because I thought Lynn was my friend. Now I am just praying to remain nonviolent, even in my thoughts about them.

What I have learned is how deeply we have been wounded as women in this society. Throughout this situation, my intention has been to try and learn from what it had to teach me. I

have tried, and failed miserably at times, to stay out of that ultimately impotent anger, which keeps one locked in a prison of
seeking revenge or seeking to hurt those who are perceived as
hurtful. Blame and counterblame is a cycle that goes nowhere.
The fact is we are all hurting, and we are all in pain, or we
would not and could not treat one another or ourselves this
way. I have learned that it does not matter if in the moment one
is in the avenger role or feeling attacked. The psychic space of
either position is poisonous, contagious, and ultimately powerless. I am speaking of true power, not power over another. I
am speaking of the power of creation, not destruction, the
power that comes when one follows one's true passion. How is
it that women choose to beat down that power in one another?

Chapter 1 contains an excerpt about aggressive girls by Judith
Sutphen. Here she offers possible explanations for why women use
RA against each other in leadership situations.

One of the most difficult aspects of being a woman leader is
relationships with other women. Women remember the
girlhood games of relational aggression well, and some
become expert players over time.

Those fleeting slights and jabs of our formative years gel
in our bones, and as adult women it feels natural, even
rewarding, to undermine, to judge, or to simply exclude
other women, especially those with ambition. We are so
good at it. Perhaps the most pernicious aspect of relational
aggression is its covert nature. Public or on-the-record comment is exposed to the air and light of public observation,
and can be accepted or dismissed by others. Covert judgment, snide remarks whispered among women, the quick
quiet side-step to avoid a show of support, can make a
woman leader feel as if she is fighting ghosts, pulling her
down by the hem of her skirt. These clinging spirits will neither release their grip nor make themselves visible.

Women don't support other women to strive for public
power out of their own oppression. Power, like aggression,
is still a dirty word for females and they remain frightened
of it. The ability of some women to be in charge, speak in a

crowd, change laws, get rich, terrifies other women to the core. Powerful women are scary to men and women alike, but for different reasons.

I recently learned of a psychology experiment in which women and men were asked to divide ten dollars in any way between themselves and another person, identified only by a gender-specific name. Men offered women less money than they did men. SO DID WOMEN. Females no less than males buy into the assumptions of a culture that values women less.

In a similar manner, men and women find it more comfortable for a man to be in charge if only because it's more familiar. Women who are bold enough to step into public life through politics or the media are often most harshly critiqued by their own gender and held to a higher standard than men.

Men can find powerful women threatening because they assume power is a zero sum game. If you have power there's less for me. Women know this isn't true, but powerful women show them too much about themselves, and they instinctively turn away from this knowledge. When a woman aspires to public respect and influence, i.e., public power, it conveys to other women that this avenue might be available for them also. If they choose to not ally themselves to her, in fact to undermine her ambitions, then they don't have to consider what her aspirations say about themselves and their life choices.

It's time for women to acknowledge and bring into public discourse those girlish games of relational aggression and its pernicious effects on our adult lives. When women recognize and truly embrace what they themselves have to offer as individuals, the ambition of other women will no longer threaten them. Only when women fully support the aspirations of their own gender will other women dare to step up into the limelight, which is big enough to hold us all.

Although the incident that follows did not take place in a work setting, it did occur between two women in the same profession, who presumably would be colleagues. Eager for mutual exchange, the author reached out to a fellow writer and was stung by the RA-type behaviors she received.

Encounter with a Sister
ELAYNE CLIFT

I recognize her immediately. She is a feminist writer and social critic, and her latest book has been well-received and enlightening. In spite of myself, I feel a wave of excitement at the thought that we are seat mates on the long flight from Beijing to Tokyo, but I try to remember that I, too, am a writer who has been covering the Fourth World Conference on Women, and that makes us equals to some degree.

I try to strike up a conversation, but immediately she begins to interrogate me, notebook in hand. It is clear that I am merely another subject and not a colleague as, periodically, she smiles condescendingly at me and nods to her friend, who occupies the third seat, in a knowing, isn't-that-interesting kind of way. What did I think? she asks. How did I know that? Where was I when . . . ? Like a remnant with potential, she rolls me around in her brain, turns me upside down to explore my crevassed perceptions, runs her mind over my experience so as to help shape her own. Then, extraction complete, she closes her notebook and eats lunch.

I try to remain composed and act the journalist myself, but she is having none of it. She is not the least bit interested in my questions; she has no desire to share her own perceptions with me. She has gotten what she wants; there is no further need for exchange.

Later, in place of friendship, I offer her a copy of my book, because she is quoted there.

"I don't have time to read," she says. "So much to write!" All she really needed to say was "Thank you," even if she then tossed my work in the trash.

At the airport, we melt into immigration, she in one line, and me in another. They may as well have been marked "Famous Feminist" and "Anonymous."

The irony of the situation is not lost on me. We both went to Beijing to listen, to hear women's voices forty thousand strong, to share, to learn. Inclusion was supposedly our mantra, diversity our jewel. We are contemporaries, she and I, writers and women of a certain age and point of view. We might have had a real conversation, shared impressions and ideas. Instead, having gained nothing, she turned from me, precious notebook in hand.

Once again, a harsh lesson is forced upon me: the feminism to which I am deeply wedded is vital, but it has its prima donnas, and their bad behavior is never justified. Their politically-saturated egos will never replace human kindness in the everyday events of life. What's more, curiosity should never trump courtesy, Famous Feminist or not.

Perhaps something of what I said on that flight in 1995 actually made it into the writer's copy; I'll never know. This much I do know: that woman made it onto my blacklist, and there she will remain. It's one of the sadder legacies of an event that was meant to stand for solidarity and sisterhood, no matter how many bylines we may have.

Feminists are not alone in their mistreatment of the very group they hope to empower; other female-oriented work situations suffer from the same issues. The many communications I received from nurses, therapists, and other medical professionals discussed adversarial relationships they encountered among women in the workplace.

The Healers

Members of the healing professions are usually described as caring and compassionate, two qualities traditionally associated with the female gender. In careers such as nursing, counseling, and, increasingly, medicine, groups of women must associate with one another an intense physical and emotional basis, usually in an effort to help and heal others. Given the shared goal and close environment, can these professions avoid the destructive RA dynamic?

In a recent meeting, a female physician who worked closely with a group of nurses told me, "The nurses—they are like sisters. You can tell they get along really well." There was a wistfulness to her words that made me wish I, too, could be part of that group of women who worked so well and so intimately. A short time later, I spoke with a nurse who had just resigned from her job. "What bitches!" she exclaimed bitterly, referring to her former coworkers. "I have never experienced anything like it since high school. The bickering and backbiting and fighting were phenomenal."

The latter incident is far more representative of what I was told by female physicians and nurses. They suggest that RA is just as prevalent in hospitals and other organizations dedicated to health care as in the settings discussed previously. Kate, a middle-aged pediatrician at a large university hospital, recalls the following:

> When I was in medical school there were only a handful of other women, all of them better qualified than the men in their class in that they got better grades and worked harder at academics. Even in residency, which is very competitive, we were collegial. Bullying wasn't much of an issue.
>
> In practice I have now found control issues, certainly. A clinical nurse manager did things to me that she wouldn't do to a male physician. I had problems with things like not being able to schedule clinic time, not scheduling patients, taking time slots from my clinic time without discussion. It's been resolved, after discussion, so the person was amenable to change.
>
> I think the feelings of powerlessness and overwork make women cruel to each other. My division chief is excellent at resolving conflict. He's very fair. I think it would help if women had someone to go to and discuss problems in a neutral atmosphere. Creating an atmosphere where open communication is valued is important.
>
> Our social worker has fostered an environment for a common cause, instead of competition, so it's much less acceptable to act aggressively. I have seen in other departments how zingers go back and forth in the guise of humor, but that doesn't go on where I work. He (our social worker) fosters an attitude of, "We're here for the patient." When people get frustrated or start controlling, the common goal to work for the patient helps to lessen the frustration. We find that when we ask, "What's best for this patient?" it depersonalizes the conflict.

Carole, a general practitioner in the Northeast, echoes feelings of closeness with other female physicians, but discord with nurses.

In medical school, I had positive relationships with my peers for the most part. There were some situations where people viewed you as a competitor instead of a friend. I made friends with a woman who had moved away from her family to go to medical school. My husband and I took her in—she became part of the family. I found out she was stealing from me! I kept thinking I was losing things when one of the other students told me to wake up and smell the coffee. She was definitely sabotaging my success.

In residency, I made some of my best female friends. I didn't have any negative relationships. We were more into survival than being competitive. We had such long hours and were so tired, you just needed to stick together. We were just treated poorly as a group.

The nurses see you as uppity, because as a physician you have to write orders, which means more work for the nurses. There were a few nurses, mostly older women who had been around for a long time, who felt free to threaten me by saying, "I've been here for thirty years and . . ." They were caring and considerate of how they treated other people, but had more of a condescending attitude toward residents. If they made suggestions and I wouldn't take them, I always felt obligated to explain my reasoning to them, and that was true of other women residents. Our male counterparts didn't explain their reasoning. Females have a tendency to question female authority, but it's generally a positive thing because it adds to the team spirit.

I was chosen as one of four chief residents in my last year of residency. I had an experience with a woman who was one of the other chief residents when I made a decision she didn't agree with. I had made this decision easily, keeping the patient's care in mind, but she perceived me as being lazy. She took it upon herself to reprimand me even though we were equals. I was so stunned I couldn't respond. She had complete comfort with reprimanding, but she did it in a passive-aggressive manner. My trust level for her was very low the rest of the year. How ridiculous it was, but I've never been able to forgive. In the final analysis, it's an issue of trust. Any decision I made from then on, I felt she was looking over my shoulder. She defended her bad behavior in the name of friendship with the head chief resident.

I'm part of the problem. For the most part, until that point, I never had to be aggressive with other people. It was my first major decision and my hormones didn't help. I was fatigued and pregnant, and I just came off a service of working up to a hundred hours a week.

Our male colleague exploded when he found out what she had done to me. It's much healthier to react that way, I'm sure. I think that I need to digest things, since I'm not comfortable with making quick comebacks. I always regret knee-jerk responses.

At this point of my career, where I am now, I try very hard to be perceived as equal with women who aren't physicians. I use my first name rather than the doctor title. I think women are cruel to each other because it's safer to be cruel to someone of your own gender. Generally, it isn't safe to do it to men.

More than one nurse has indicated agreement with the belief that nurses are especially cruel to novices. Several wrote to share RA experiences they had with coworkers. Ginny was one who felt disillusioned with her choice of career and captured the feelings of many.

Oh, my! The nursing profession! I have been in it for seventeen years. I was nineteen when I started working in a local hospital where I was loved and nurtured. God blessed me with that job. After two years, I took a position with another local hospital because I was getting married, and it was closer to my husband's place of employment. There wasn't much nurturing there, but I have always felt that the nursing profession does eat its young! Over the years there continues to be backstabbing, gossiping, rumor starting, eye rolling, whispering, and exclusion. One LPN always feels that she gets the heaviest load. One RN always gives her a heavy assignment, because she feels this LPN doesn't work as hard as others do, answering bells and helping others. The three-to-eleven shift probably has the most rumor starting, gossiping and relational aggression in general, because it is the most short-staffed and usually has the youngest nurses in the profession.

We even have a nursing supervisor who exhibits relational aggression all the time. It is not uncommon for someone to say, "She is stirring the trouble pot again." She loves to gossip. Some of us blow off her comments and don't repeat them, knowing what she is trying to do and hoping to stop it before it gets started. Thankfully, some of us will continue to follow the Golden Rule.

Having known many psychotherapists, I naively believed women within this profession would be kinder role models for us all. Not so. I received this account from Patricia Ferguson, Psy.D., a clinical psychologist, who wrote:

For the most part, my general, adult female relationships have been good in spite of moving around the country several times. For ten years, I have lived in a town where two women inflicted great emotional harm. My husband warned me about one of them many times, but I naively ignored him.

I think I wanted a relationship with these women because we were all psychotherapists with the same values and beliefs, as well as much in common. My relationship with each of them was different, but each would talk about the other behind her back, which should have warned me that they talked about me, too. I should never have allowed such conversations to continue, and I can see now it was just the junior high school triangle.

I was the only one with a doctorate, and I think they thought my practice was the most successful, which may have been true. They were also jealous because men would comment on how young I looked when, in fact, I was the same age as one of them.

The three of us were part of a small group of women who spent time together at work and with our families. However, it seemed my family would always be with one or the other of theirs, never all three together. We were also split at work: two of us worked in the same office because I had helped her get space there.

The specifics of our breakup are irrelevant, but I now see it was inevitable. What is worth mentioning is that they gossiped about me during a time when I was having significant personal problems and needed friends to come through and be supportive. One of the women convinced the other woman (the one who was my age) that they should end their relationship with me, and so, in a single phone call, it was over.

Interestingly, they tried to continue to be friends with my husband. I told him how hurtful it was that they would hold a conversation with him as if I weren't standing there right next to him. Now neither of them speaks to us, even though we live in a small town and see each other frequently.

The stressors that led up to the end are over, but the interesting thing is that the people who come through for you are never the ones you expect to, while others you count on take off.

I know I share responsibility for what happened. I shouldn't have allowed the abuse to continue beyond one incident with both of them. Therapists can be the worst friends to each other, which is something that I learned was true for others while I was in training.

Another therapist described an extreme degree of professional jealousy and competition that was more pronounced in women than in men. She encountered these issues again and again, especially at conferences where a critical mass of psychologists gathered and often ended up comparing notes. Inevitably, the women were more competitive and caustic in their comments than the men.

When We're Good, We're Very Good

If all female-dominated organizations functioned in such a destructive fashion, it would seem a hopeless ideal to strive for RA-free environments. Yet in some circumstances, female-led organizations can not only work well, they can be a source of great satisfaction and empowerment to everyone involved.

Sheri McConnell is the founder and president of the National Alliance of Women Writers (NAWW). She has a graduate degree in organizational management and is a social worker who talks about her experiences with RA.

RA is dependent on people, their situations, their phases of life, and stress levels. I'm in relationships where we are helping each other as writers. I'll get mean e-mails because someone is having a bad day, and I know it's not about me, it's about them. Certain people do exist a whole lifetime in that mode. They get stuck. Other people grow from adversity.

When I first started NAWW, I was networking in discussion groups, and one in particular got into toxic things about nothing, so I stopped. I learned interdependence from [the author] Steven Covey. Bringing other people in helps us come up with better ideas.

Women do have the pecking order, but there's two ends of the spectrum. We can go anywhere and start up a conversation based on intuition. Within two or three sentences, we can share experiences. For me, I can connect with just about any woman. That's why I built a woman's group.

I think my success in connecting women has to do with my social work personality. In our groups that meet once a month, the first couple of years, we would have different personalities come in, and I wouldn't allow anyone to be negative. If you are really nice and helpful, others will follow your lead. Sometimes people didn't come back, because they didn't fit in with that. I've been to conferences where your writing is used to get at you, and some really critique your work harshly. Some people have that style, out of fear of their own inadequacies. But NAWW pretty much doesn't have anything to do with that. We have about sixty people in the online writing critique, and they've all been positive. I would cut someone off if she was negative. If someone says something toxic, I delete it.

My advice is to reach out and learn from each other. Benefit. You get what you give. You have to reaffirm that.

Sheri is just one example of a woman who draws on female strengths to build a powerful network. Consider these organizations:

- The Wild Women of Wonder (WiWoWo) consists of approximately twenty-five businesswomen who gather to network and empower one another. The corporate power of this group is respected throughout the Silicon Valley (www.fortune.com).

- The Radnor Girls Group is a group of entrepreneurs from the Philadelphia area who have joined forces to share leads and opportunities with other women seeking to start their own business (www.fortune.com).

- eWomenNetwork Inc. (www.ewomennetwork.com) is a Dallas-based Internet organization that offers a wealth of online resources for businesswomen. The group also offers a weekly radio show on issues related to women in the workplace.

There are many women leaders who have built their careers on principles of empowering other women: the talk-show host and philanthropist Oprah Winfrey, the astronaut Sally Ride, Avon CEO and chairman Andrea Jung, the Olympic athlete Jackie Joyner Kersee, the philanthropist and breast cancer advocate Susan Komen, the cosmetic maven Mary Kay, the world champion soccer player Mia Hamm, the businesswoman Kate White (author of *Why Good Girls Don't Get Ahead but Gutsy Girls Do: Nine Secrets Every Working Woman Must Know*), and many more. The examples these women provide of the positive power of female connections make the need to transform RA relationships even more critical.

Women's Words of Wisdom

In the world of work, women seem to focus on the twin values of acceptance and process, with physicians feeling a need to justify their actions to female coworkers and feminists expecting their organizations to be more humanistic than those dominated by men because women are the majority. These beliefs may inadvertently create a climate conducive to RA. By coincidence, shortly before completing the final edits for this book the subject of relational aggression came up in the medical humanities elective "Physicians and Nurses" that I teach. While I didn't point out that the dynamic we were discussing was RA, the comments about relationships between female medical students and nurses clearly resonated with issues described in this chapter. Women in the group clearly felt their male counterparts got treated better by nurses than they did, and even female nursing students agreed their peers were likely to give preferential treatment to men, whether they were doctors or nurses.

It seems that there needs to be more explicit discussion and acknowledgment of RA between and among women who are concerned with the treatment of women. Each situation written about here, although painful, also offers an opportunity for learning, understanding, and even change.

Based on the words of the women who wrote the stories contained in this chapter, recognizing and dealing with conflict among women at work is crucial, because the victim-aggressor dynamic can become endemic, especially in organizations where the ethic is equality. An emphasis on shared goals, whether for a certain committee structure or a patient care plan, can help women focus on issues other than personal relationships and power struggles.

The importance of treating all women with respect is vital, especially for women who have identified themselves as feminists. In every encounter, recognition and acceptance of another woman's abilities and interests is common courtesy. She need not become your best friend, or even any kind of friend, but the occasion to communicate with a like-minded woman, be it in an airplane, in an elevator, or as you sit in a waiting room, should be treated with courtesy.

Power is clearly an underlying struggle for women who interact aggressively in the workplace: the Queen Bee is determined to get it and maintain it, the Middle Bee may be reluctant to claim it for herself, and the Afraid-to-Bee is often frustrated by her sense of hopelessness and lack of any control. Other contributors have more to say about the power dynamic, but as Judith Sutphen points out, power does not have limits. One woman's gain should be every woman's gain, rather than a source of envy or loss. Neema Caughran, the former executive director of women's commission, sums up the issue nicely: true power comes from passion, not aggression.

CHAPTER 8

Sharing Space
Ages and Stages of Aggression

*Wanted: female roommate to share one-bedroom
apartment. Must be nonsmoker, quiet, considerate of
others, and dependable. References required!*

—AN AD POSTED ON A PUBLIC BULLETIN BOARD

At certain times of life, women are likely to live together—
either as young adults in school or in the early stages of
careers and again in the later years. This begs the question: when
quarters are close, is RA more or less intense? Some of my professional experiences come to mind when I consider this question.

There's No Place Like Home

During one of my clinical placements when I was training to be a
nurse practitioner, I ran a clinic in a high-rise apartment complex
for older, mostly women, adults. I remember how jolly the groups
of elderly ladies were who left early each morning for exercise
classes or shopping trips, and I even joked with my best friend
about how she and I might one day find ourselves in a similar
place. But were my perceptions accurate, or were there just as
many unhappy women sitting in their apartments, excluded by the
cliques I saw?

In the same way, my years as a professor have brought me in
frequent contact with college-aged women. While watching them
throwing a Frisbee or sunbathing en masse, aggression seems like

the furthest thing from their minds. Yet I know these same relationships can take on darker sides for girls who can't make friends
or those who quickly wear out friends.

Conventional wisdom suggests that RA peaks during the
middle school years and tapers off a bit in high school, but the
stories I received for this book show it is alive and well between
the ages of thirty and fifty. But what about younger and older
adult women? In these two groups, interactions with female
peers may be more intense than at any other time of life because
living arrangements can be so physically close. Are college students and young adults too busy establishing themselves to
engage in such destructive behaviors? In the same way, do older
women outgrow RA, especially during the years when women
outnumber men and there simply aren't as many options for
companionship?

To answer these questions, I solicited input from women in age
extremes, defining RA and then asking if the behaviors were familiar to them and how they manifested in various situations.

Does RA Exist in Higher Education?

Several female students at different universities provided surprisingly candid opinions on how RA plays out in their lives. Each was
asked to comment on behaviors used to hurt another and given a
list of examples (provided by a college senior familiar with RA).
The examples included name calling; passing nasty notes; making
fun of someone by rolling your eyes or making disparaging
sounds; bumping into someone on purpose; taunting someone;
damaging someone's property; making fun of someone's clothes,
appearance, or weight; instant messaging rumors and gossip;
getting friends to exclude someone you are mad at; revealing
someone's secrets; talking behind someone's back; making mean
jokes and then saying "just kidding"; and spreading rumors and
telling gossip.

All of the young women agreed that RA was a frequent occur-
rence and suggested that the use of such behaviors might even
escalate during the college years. The following are selections
from their comments:

There is so much pressure to be popular, to have a boyfriend, to get good grades, and so on, and people tend to make fun of each other out of jealousy. Popular girls are the worst, because they think they are better than everyone else and have the right to make fun of other people. Sorority girls can be very guilty of this, too. I have been involved as bully, victim, and bystander. I am definitely guilty of making fun of people or gossiping in class, but I have also been the one who has been made fun of as well. Girls always compete with each other, for boys, attention, and so on—it goes on in my house all the time. I have also listened to others bully people or make fun of them, but I stood up for the victims. If everyone treated people or talked about people like they would want to be treated or talked about, the world would be a better place.

—Crystal, college senior

Relational aggression does go on in college, but in a more premeditated way so that it is not plainly obvious who is at fault for starting rumors, making accusations, and so on. Individuals who find that this behavior gets them what they want and don't have the conscience to persuade them otherwise develop the ability to hurt others for their own personal gain, while learning sneakier methods to mask their responsibility.

Girls with low self-esteem are more likely to be involved in RA because they do not have enough confidence in themselves to deal with problems. They point their fingers and blame others to make the problems their fault, instead of finding productive ways to deal with them. They also cause a lot of unnecessary drama and hurt while never actually solving the problems.

—Tracy, college junior

I don't think anyone is free from being an aggressor. It's human nature to react when you are annoyed by a drama queen, threatened by someone hitting on your boyfriend, or have a bad day and take it out on someone with less fashion sense than you. But a line is crossed when it becomes a malicious pattern. I've seen this happen to a friend of mine who was caught in a compromising position with a guy who had a girlfriend that my friend was a casual acquaintance with. All the friends of that girl went out of their way to make her an outcast from their group. Interestingly enough, the guy was not put through any of the ridicule.

I think a lot of it happens because of alcohol. People do all sorts of things they normally wouldn't when they are drunk and more misunderstandings occur because people are not thinking straight.

—Anonymous, college senior

It's interesting and ironic that competition and/or disloyalty around a man prompts almost identical RA behaviors in coeds as it does in the adolescent girls I work with through Club and Camp Ophelia. Even more remarkable is that when these situations occur, both age groups retaliate exclusively against the woman, even if the man or boy involved is just as guilty of misconduct.

Aggression *absolutely* occurs all the time in college, especially gossiping. I have participated in gossiping, jealousy, and so on; however, I'm not proud of it, because I also know how it feels to be on the other end of it. I think RA occurs in every group of women, because each human being has flaws. No one is perfect. We see things we want, characteristics we wish we had, people we admire, qualities we desire, and we allow that to get the best of us. One thing that we can do to prevent it is when we hear gossiping, don't participate in it and encourage others to do the same. And next time you find yourself talking about someone else, stop and ask, "If that person were here, would she be offended that I'm saying this about her?" Try and see things from an outside perspective.

—Andrea, college sophomore

I can see how relational aggression might continue on in college due to sororities and organizations such as those. Sororities come across as very large cliques, and it is no secret that these organizations haze and encourage alcohol use as a means to measure how dedicated a person is to the group and the likelihood that the person will be accepted into the group. I have participated in hazing both as a so-called victim and a bystander. When I was involved, though, I never felt like I was being bullied or manipulated. It was all in fun. There were certain things I felt uncomfortable doing and I said so; no one made me do anything I didn't want to do. In the same respect, when it was me watching someone else tell people what to do, I reiterated the fact that they didn't have to do anything they didn't want to. A way to prevent RA is simply standing up for your beliefs. I feel that we are all past the point of peer pressure and can make our own rational, responsible decisions. If an outsider notices such actions, they should stand up as well. No one should stand alone, and we can all use the help and support of others.

—Alicia, college senior

Relational aggression definitely goes on at my small school, but I know it goes on at bigger universities, too, just to different degrees. I've been a victim, and I've been a bystander, because my friends constantly make fun of people for some reason or another, and, of course, I've been an aggressor, too. I don't know many people who can plead completely innocent. Rumors are very involved in this little place.

I think it happens here because it's a small college on a small campus and easy to know everyone on a more personal level. To prevent it, call it in the act, even if it's your friends participating. They'll respect your opinion more than the possible retaliation of the person being picked on.

—Lauren, college senior

Jealousy, cliques, and gossip are big behaviors I notice. I'm sure I have been involved in all three scenarios during my college career. I know with my group of friends this happens because we judge people based on what they are wearing, or who they are hanging out with, because it gives us all something to talk about and share common opinions. I don't know if we do it to make ourselves feel better, but usually we do it to people younger than us. I really do not know how to prevent this from happening. Girls seem to have a natural desire to always be competing with one another and that usually causes RA to occur.

—Elly, college senior

I think relational aggression continues throughout a woman's life. It doesn't just end after high school or college but continues in the workforce and social groups of adult women as well. Females by nature are catty and petty; it is a rare thing to find a girl who has never made fun of someone or spread a rumor. I have been involved as a victim; people have made fun of me, talked about me behind my back, revealed my secrets, and I have done the same. I am a sarcastic person, and I always make rude jokes and then say, "Just kidding." I also spread gossip and talk about people behind their backs. I don't think I have a single friend who has not participated in some of these actions. It is a way to break the ice in a situation where a woman might feel vulnerable and in need of acceptance. It is a way to make one feel better about one's self, pointing out the faults of another. It is immature and rude, but it's a part of life. It makes life interesting, spices things, creates drama, and makes an otherwise dull situation livelier.

All girls participate in RA. Certain types of girls, such as popular, attractive, sorority girls, may be more prone to these actions because they enjoy pointing out ways that they are better than others. It gives these girls something to talk about when they have nothing better to do, but this is a problem that all women contribute to in some shape or form.

—Helen, college senior

It definitely does go on. I've only been a victim when alcohol is involved. I believe most college students can say the same, because alcohol is so available in college. I have also been an aggressor. At parties, when girls can be rude, I'll be rude back. When drinking, people lose their inhibitions and tend to say or do what they feel, even if it hurts another. To prevent it, I think people should think how they would feel if someone was doing or saying the same to them. Also to lessen the chances of RA happening, one can abstain from drinking.

I used to feel that attractiveness, wealth, and intelligence made people feel they were superior enough to engage in RA; however, I found that that is simply a stereotype. In college, I have friends who fall into all of those categories and they are some of the nicest people in the world. Therefore, I feel the main variable in RA is simply insecurity.

—Jacki, college junior

I think there are a lot of reasons why RA happens. One of the main reasons is that in college everyone lives together. In high school you see your friends a lot, but it's not the same as living in the same dorm or apartment as them. It's a lot easier to get on someone's nerves, and people get annoyed with each other more often when living together. Also, in college people are exposed to a lot of people who are different from them and unlike people they knew back home. Sometimes there is jealousy about lifestyles or ignorance about someone from a different culture that can be a cause of aggression. It is easy to say that attractive and wealthy girls are more snotty or are meaner to people, but that's also a form of RA as well. I think that by stereotyping entire groups of people we would be doing the same thing to them as we claim they are doing to other people.

I don't think there is much that we can do to prevent it besides monitoring our own behavior and being more conscious of what we do. Sometimes it's easier to be mean and do hurtful things than it is to work out a problem, and I think people have to be willing to put in the effort and risk having an uncomfortable confrontation to work their problems out.

—Anonymous, college junior

In college RA gets worse because you realize, more than in high school, that it is time to search for a mate.

—Trudy, college sophomore

Perhaps the college years are an unusual time when women live closely together before launching their adult lives. If this is the case, "mature" women at the other end of the spectrum might be expected to outgrow RA. After a lifetime of relationships, do women finally come to understand and practice relational affection rather than relational aggression?

Too Old to Aggress?

During my years in clinical geriatrics, I observed many women in situations where they shared living space, often in the same way as college students. Sometimes this arrangement seemed to work well, as in the high-rise apartment complex I described earlier. In other situations, I saw cliques in nursing homes where I worked and judgmental, hurtful behaviors among women residents in assisted living centers, almost identical to the actions of some of the middle schoolers in my programs for girls. Still, these are only my observations. To explore how older women themselves perceive these issues, I found several who were willing to talk to me about the subject.

Mabel, who is eighty-three, lives alone in a retirement community.

In school, I was too busy with chores and other things to have close relationships, so that wasn't my way. But I have had friends. When I was in my thirties, I had my family, and I was very involved with them, but I would say I am more involved with friends now. I'm easy to get along with, but I'm not the outgoing type. I'm definitely more of a listener.

I'm not the type of person to talk about other people and never have been. Here, there is a problem if women live in close proximity. Some of my friends and I get meals together, and they get to talking about other women while we eat. Sometimes I think maybe they're so involved in themselves, and they need something else to get involved in. I would say it does go on with some women and not others.

If there is gossip, I don't participate. I was just in a situation like that and was so thankful that I didn't have those problems. I have seen jealousy around someone having a husband, and exclusion around being married or not. You could be in or out of a group for this reason.

Tam Gray, age sixty-seven, was a reporter for *Time* magazine and founder of the Web site www. seniorwomen.com. She has a network of female colleagues that extends across the country and is a recognized expert on older women's issues. Many postings on her Web site deal with relationships, but more often they concern relationships with children and parents than friends.

Being married creates less need for women to find and sustain relationships with each other, but widowhood changes that.

I find that friendships with women do not last in many cases as long as friendships with men. Men are less volatile in how they treat relationships. They don't get disappointed as quickly. My attitudes toward friendship with women started when I was five years old. All of a sudden your friends want to criticize each other. I'm not sure men would ever think of doing something like that. It would break down something for them that is hard to build. I think for men it's much harder to form relationships that have any depth.

Women can start relationships very quickly, but then we get too much into people's lives and are too interested in details of other women's lives. Women are so curious. We want to find out how other females work. We all ask those kinds of questions: how did you meet your husband, where did you go to school, and so on. We start digging, digging, digging, in order to see how safe that other woman is, in order to make a friend of her. You wonder: Will she be there for you? Does she have her own agenda?

Maybe it's instinctual. When my husband and I meet someone, I will say, "Gee, I think she is blah, blah, blah," and my husband won't even have noticed. Women's intuition has more of a reality base than we think it does.

Another older woman describes her friendship experience in the later years in the following story.

Looking for a Female Friend

B. B. Carter

If you're sixty-two years old, newly divorced, and have just moved to another state away from family and friends, you come to realize that you're a traumatized nervous wreck.

Suicide is not an option, because you're afraid your children would hate you and refuse to visit the cemetery. Antidepressants, sleeping pills, and gallons of Ben and Jerry's ice cream don't make you feel any better. So what do you finally do? You search for a few new female friends.

A couple of months ago, I finally got my act together and decided to stop feeling sorry for myself and do something positive about my sorrowful life. I realized the first step I had to take was to make some new, single, female friends who had similar interests to mine.

Most women get on the Internet and look for a man, but not me. I clicked on "Women Looking for Men," and searched for a few single women who said they loved "writing, dancing, theatre" and other things I enjoyed. I wrote to two of them, describing myself and telling them I was looking to make new women friends because I was single and new to the area. I enclosed my phone number and suggested we start a writing workshop.

The very first evening I received a call from Sandi. Of course, the first thing she asked was if I was a lesbian. Her question took me aback for a moment, but I finally burst out laughing and told her my sad story. The second call I got was from Sue, and when she asked me if I was gay, I laughed and told her I wasn't gay but happy she called.

A couple of days later the three of us got together for coffee and we hit it off. Before you knew it, the two of them were also searching for other women the way I did, and we're now a group of twelve single women. Who says the Internet doesn't work? We're not only good friends, but we support each other on bad days, make sure that none of us are left with nothing to do on holidays or Saturday nights. Oh yes—I no longer have to drown myself in ice cream. I'm far too busy for that.

Women's Words of Wisdom

The news about aggression can be discouraging if the prevalence of such behaviors is all we focus on. The perceptions and suggestions of the women in this chapter, however, are valuable because they promote a better understanding of RA and how certain environments, such as closely shared space in an all-female setting, may create a risk for such behaviors.

The ability of young women to recognize RA as a mask for low self-esteem and insecurity that helps depersonalize behaviors is impressive. Their identification of alcohol as a risk factor for aggressive exchanges and the suggestion to reduce RA by avoiding inebriation also has the potential to reduce these behaviors. The realization that assumptions and stereotypes of other women can trigger RA-type behaviors is also valuable, as is the suggestion to make a policy of treating others as you would like to be treated. This Golden Rule for relationships would include a zero tolerance policy for gossip and other damaging behaviors, which older women affirmed as well.

There is a value in acknowledging the gamut of behaviors younger women use to wound one another because it forces us to realize that even teasing or pretending to be joking when delivering hurtful comments is, in fact, a destructive way of interacting. Retaliating against a woman who cheats with your boyfriend while excusing his behavior is another inconsistent action recognized as RA by the younger women.

Equally interesting observations about the nature of women and the joy of positive connections came from the older women who contributed to this chapter. Knowing which behaviors contribute to positive female companionship may not end RA, but it can help us approach and celebrate relationships from a different perspective. As Tam Gray pointed out, women are able to establish connections much more quickly than men, often because they enter personally loaded territory more readily. This can be promising or problematic.

No book on women would be complete without an affirmation of the benefits of a female support group. The need to enjoy rather than undermine our attachments to one another was one of my motivations for writing this book. B. B. Carter's story is proof that positive connections with women can be one of the most healing and enriching forces in our lives.

CHAPTER 9

Forced to Be Family
The Good, the Bad, and the Very Ugly of Female In-Laws

My sisters and I can't stand her, but she's my brother's
wife, so there's no choice. We have to pretend to be nice.
—DENISE, ONE OF FOUR SISTERS WHOSE BROTHER
IS MARRIED TO A WOMAN NONE OF THEM LIKE

Through marriage, we inherit mothers and sisters we may not choose as friends in other circumstances. Many women find this an opportunity to develop relationships they might have wanted during childhood or in their family of origin but never had. Frequently, the friendship of a sister-in-law or the love of a mother-in-law was cherished by women, and there were as many positive stories contributed on this topic as there were negative.

When stories were negative, though, they seemed more intense than in any other situation where women group together. Perhaps forced contact with the mother or sister of your husband by virtue of marriage creates circumstances of extreme RA, especially when these contacts occur during holidays, a time when tensions normally are heightened.

Dr. Neema Caugheran, whose story appeared earlier, also studies relationships between women connected by marriage. She points out that:

In very patriarchal societies, it is women who are the enforcers of their own oppression. In traditional Hindu society where a young woman goes to live with her husband's family, she becomes like a slave. It is the mother-in-law who might beat her into submission or starve her to gain control. These women have never had any power, they were once daughters-in-law, beaten, starved, abused, and those who carry on this behavior cannot help themselves; it is their turn now. It is not personal; it is simply the only way known through experience. Women all over the world were and are somehow conditioned to treat each other without real respect. Women were and are somehow conditioned to enforce the rules of the patriarchy, which taught that power shall not rest in the hands of women.

When I was a victim of female aggression, I realized that the vendetta of the women involved ultimately didn't have anything to do with me. The roots of their behavior were deeper. They were simply carrying on the work of upholding the system of oppression, taking out their own wounds on other women. When women do these things, we are often unconscious that is what we are doing. Our wounds may not be physical; we do not starve or beat each other. Yet, we are wounded in our ability to have respect for each other's wisdom and experience. We are wounded in our ability to have compassion for one another. But most importantly, in this kind of destructive mind-set, we are wounded in our ability to have compassion for ourselves. We are taught to take care of everyone else, and we are also taught that we dare not take care of ourselves and of each other. This is a wound of spirit.

License to Hurt

The Internet is rife with stories of in-law aggression, always between females and always relational. Like the correspondence I received, many women complained of Queen Bee sisters- or mothers-in-law who manipulate, exclude, and intimidate them.

The offenses ranged from stealing the name intended for a child to pushing grandparents to favor one set of children or grand-children over another.

Afraid-to-Bee victims are subjected to criticism from their female in-laws on parenting skills, homemaking abilities, physical appearances, work ethics, and a number of other attributes. There seems to be little recourse for handling this aggression, because any action perceived as retaliation might endanger a spouse's relationships with his family.

Consider these situations, which were posted on various Web sites:

- On www.babycenter.com, a young mother asked for help because her sister-in-law used her as a free babysitter, drop-ping her child off without notice. Numerous replies indi-cated that many women grapple with this problem. Some resolved it with return aggression, and others took no action in an effort to preserve family relationships.

- On the ezboard site "bitches" (http://p199.ezboard.com/ fbitchpillowfamilybitch) there were several postings. One titled "The sister-in-law from hell" ("I am so happy I found this site. I randomly typed in 'bitchy sister-in-law' and this site came up. . . . My sister-in-law is the most manipulative bitch in the world.") described how the sister-in-law manipulated everyone in the family into believing she had been wronged and taken advantage of by the woman who wrote the post. Other posts on this site were from women who described being excluded, intimidated, or teased under the guise of "joking," and having their parents-in-law turned against them by gossip, all at the hands of sisters-in-law.

- From www.angerproject.com came a post by Lisa who said, "The only way to describe her is that she [sister-in-law] is an adult bully. She thrives on putting other people down to make herself feel better. She is verbally and some-times physically abusive to others. I know that SHE is the one with the problem, but the ugly things she says and does to me and others makes me go insane. I just can't help hating her. She is such a control freak. She's gotten away with this behavior since she's been a child because people are afraid to confront her. Our children go to the same school and our husbands are in business together. My in-laws also hate her behavior, but tell me that I just have to learn to deal with it. All of this has turned ME into a nasty person because I have so much hate inside of me." Others who responded to Lisa's post had similar negative comments about their own sisters-in-law, and little advice on what action could be taken without alienating husbands or parents-in-law.

- On www.indolink.com/Forum/Women a post about a sister-in-law problem yielded this response (excerpted):

  The solution that I think is the best in cases like this is you give them up. I mean, give up the idea of being beloved and accepted for them. Let it go. There are a lot of people that can give you love, respect and friendship, besides your husband's family.

  I came from another country and I have no family here in the USA. It makes it harder and sadder. If you have your family here, spend time w/ them, love them, cherish them, take care of your friends w/ love and respect, be w/ people that appreciate your company. . . .

  We can't force people to love us. But we can allow ourselves to be loved.

  I know it hurts. But if you surround yourself w/people who love you and let behind people who don't . . . it will make a lot of difference in your life.

These posts are vivid examples of how RA that occurs between women who are forced to be family can reach hurtful extremes.

Mothers-in-law also are often accused of aggressive behaviors toward their daughters-in-law, and vice versa. The behaviors most frequently cited are nicely summarized in the following scenario.

Unfortunate Mother-in-Law and Daughter-in-Law Dichotomies

RUTH HARRIET JACOBS, PH.D.

Special thanks to Ellie Mamber for some suggestions of the role difficulties.

MIL refers to mother-in-law

DIL refers to daughter-in-law

1. MIL: I will give DIL the benefit of my experience by giving her advice and suggestions.

   DIL: My MIL is manipulative, and her advice is rotten and outdated.

2. MIL: I hope, expect, or dread that DIL will be like my own daughter.

   DIL: I hope, expect, or dread that MIL will be like my own mother.

3. MIL: My son is unhappy because DIL is neurotic, selfish, not meeting his needs, not taking good care of him. She is worse than other DILs.

   DIL: MIL spoiled my husband so that he is neurotic, selfish, and doesn't meet my needs or take good care of me. MIL is worse than other MILs.

4. MIL: My grandchildren's problems are the fault of DIL, who didn't/does not bring them up right. My daughter is a better mother.

   DIL: My children's problems are the result of poor fathering, because MIL failed to bring up her son to be a good father. MIL also pays more attention to her daughter's children than mine.

5. MIL: DIL resents my attention to the grandchildren and tries to prevent a close relationship between them and me. She lets her mother be closer to the grandchildren.

   DIL: MIL is a bad influence on her grandchildren. I wish she would not bribe them with gifts and want to spend so much time with them. I hate when MIL criticizes the way I bring up my children or relate to them as adults.

6. MIL: I'm ashamed of DIL because of her failings, background, education, and appearance. I cannot understand how my son could have chosen this woman for his wife and I cannot completely conceal this.

   DIL: I'm ashamed of MIL because of her background, education, appearance, skills, and so on. I cannot understand how my husband could have come from this family and know MIL resents me.

7. MIL: I expect DIL to become part of my extended family and fit in.

   DIL: I expect my husband, MIL's son, to become part of my extended family and fit in.

8. MIL: I always make an effort to say the right thing, not to criticize or even make suggestions. I am always on guard.

   DIL: I think MIL is a perfectionist, secretive, and uncommunicative.

9. MIL: I find DIL's house so unappealing I keep visits short and try to see my son elsewhere.

   DIL: I thinks MIL wants to see too much of her son.

10. MIL: I'm overprotective/overbearing with my son and this affects my relationship with DIL.

    DIL: I think other MILs are too invested in their sons.

11. MIL: I'm angry with my daughter and this affects my relationship with DIL, or I compare DIL unfavorably to my own daughter.

    DIL: I'm angry with my own mother and displace this on MIL, or I compare MIL unfavorably to my own mother.

12. MIL: I think DIL has bad taste in clothes and household decoration and would like to help her be more tasteful.

    DIL: I dread when MIL gives gifts of clothes or household items, because I dislike MIL's taste. I use gifts reluctantly and only when MIL visits.

13. MIL: I think DIL is disrespectful to offer advice to someone older and wiser and I'm defensive about my lifestyle.

DIL: I think MIL's lifestyle is unhealthy, old-fashioned, or stupid and would like to help her change.

14. MIL: I think how awful it would be to be sick or frail and dependent on DIL, whose decisions or caretaking I don't trust.

DIL: I dread that MIL might need help in old age, knowing the task would fall on me, not MIL's son.

15. MIL: I want my son to spend a good deal of time and attention on me and do not want equal time with DIL.

DIL: I'm jealous of the attention my husband gives his mother, not me, and wish MIL would give me the kind of attention she gives her son.

16. MIL: I think DIL is a lousy cook, extravagant, or stingy.

DIL: I think MIL is a lousy cook, extravagant, or stingy.

BETTER SCENARIOS

MIL and DIL let go of expectations, criticisms, resentment, blaming, displacement, transfer. They try to value each other and find good qualities. They accept diverse backgrounds, different values, and generational differences, and they work at tolerance and acceptance. They do not compete for the son/husband's attention or children/grandchildren's love; it is good for children to have many people who care for them.

Both realize nobody is perfect. MIL and DIL have interests outside of their relationship and enjoy friends, colleagues, neighbors, and other people. Both MIL and DIL get satisfaction and recognition for paid or volunteer work or accomplishments. Both save their advice for people in a less loaded, less problematic relationship than their own. Both realize the stresses both women encounter in an ageist, sexist society and are supportive of each other. Both listen with empathy to each other. Both bite their tongues when necessary. Both get support from others in the same boat. Both get counseling if needed. Both stop brooding. Neither thinks the son/husband's characteristics and behavior are the fault or property of the MIL or the DIL, but that the son/husband is a human being with his own character, role, and decisions.

Sadly, some women are rendered vulnerable to manipulation and aggression from female relatives due to aging, illness, and disabilities. Having negotiated many caregiving situations in my clinical practice, I was struck by the following story, which captures a dynamic that shows how extreme hurtful behaviors can become, with an elderly woman caught between two equally determined aggressors.

Prisoner of War
SUE PACE

The bank manager wore an emerald green suit with a silk blouse—no lace. Her hair was an auburn cap and her eyes were hazel. She needed to lose twenty pounds or grow three inches. That's what she told herself every morning when getting dressed. She looked sweet, but she was a greedy bitch, and she took pride in being the youngest bank manager in the state.

Marta, the widow, was seventy-eight. Her son telephoned to wish her a happy birthday and mentioned, in a joking way, that she wasn't getting any younger. Not that he was looking for an inheritance—ha ha. Absolutely not. He called to say she should travel. Take some cruises. Have fun. Do something besides stay holed up in the old place. That's what Pop would have wanted. He couldn't get away, but her daughter-in-law would take her to lunch. Anywhere she wanted.

Marta hadn't mentioned that bad investments and thousands of lost dollars meant she'd have to sell her summer place. She hadn't told anyone except her good and dear friend, Vera, who paid attention and stroked her hand and gave educated advice.

And now there were papers to sign.

The widow and her daughter-in-law arrived at the bank together. The younger woman wore ironed jeans and a soft wool jacket in fire engine red with a Ralph Lauren silk scarf draped around her throat. Calfskin boots. Wind-blown hair cut on the bias. Very chic. Very now.

The older woman wore a purple pantsuit and black flats. A serviceable navy blue coat settled heavily on her shoulders. A large tapestry purse dangled from her arm. Her thinning white hair needed a perm. She was not chic. Not now.

The bank manager frowned when she saw Marta and the

younger woman headed her way. She had errands to run during her lunch break and also her stock broker friend to nuzzle and two drinks to tuck away.

The younger woman carried a calfskin organizer. It was champagne in color, as was her hair, her boots, and the little shapes (they looked like anchors) hiding in the folds of her scarf.

"This is my daughter-in-law," Marta said by way of introduction. "She's taking me to lunch. For my birthday. Isn't that sweet?"

The bank manager smiled brightly and didn't proffer her hand.

The widow continued. "I told her I needed to sign a few papers. I know you insist on confidentiality, but I was going to be downtown anyway. . . ." The widow's voice drifted off.

"I'm Emma," the daughter-in-law said, proffering *her* hand.

"I'm Vera, your mother-in-law's financial adviser."

"Vera?" Botox kept a frown from etching itself between her finely drawn eyebrows. "You're Vera?"

"Yes."

"But I thought Vera was a friend."

"Of course I'm a friend. This is a friendly bank."

The widow began twisting her purse handles. "You're mad at me," she said. "It's so hard to get down here, and I thought just this once. I'm sorry. It won't happen again."

"What won't happen again?" Emma asked.

"Nothing to worry about," Vera said. She patted the widow's hand. "We'll do it another time."

"You'll do what another time?" Emma's voice was sharp.

"I'm supposed to sign some papers," the widow explained.

"Oh, not now," Vera said brightly. "It's your birthday. Come in tomorrow."

"What papers?" Emma was insistent.

The widow tilted her head and smiled. "Vera's such a lamb. She put together a financial plan for me, but it means I have to make a teeny-tiny change in my will."

"Does Richard know about this?" All signs of politeness had fled from Emma.

"It's *my* money," the old woman said. "I can do what I want with it."

"Of course you can," both women said in unison.

The telephone rang. Vera ignored it as long as she could but finally had to answer because all the clerks were pretending to be busy.

"We should have lunch," Emma whispered to the widow, her voice sly. "Richard will be there. It was supposed to be a surprise."

"Oh! How lovely!"

Vera saw, then, that she would lose the summer place. Emma had a cell phone. The son (who claimed over and over to have no interest in his inheritance) would show up and do what he was told.

The two bitches (bank manager and daughter-in-law) smiled coldly at each other before the widow—like a broken POW in a 1950s war movie—changed sides.

The RA behaviors between two females in a position of power (daughter-in-law and bank manager) made this elderly woman a double victim, betrayed by both a family member and a trusted confident.

This following note from Pat, a female caregiver, describes a different but common type of aggression: the caregiver put-down.

Relational aggression with female relations is yet another matter. I used to quake in my boots when a particularly domineering cousin would call to harangue me about filial responsibilities related to the care of my beloved mother, who lived with me for the last five years of her life. When my mother lay on her deathbed, this individual phoned me in the hospital to discourage the choice of cremation (my mother's wish) and made every effort to persuade me to buy a burial plot next to her mother's plot in a remote country cemetery. To this day, I face every telephone conversation with this bullying cousin, now in her sixties, with fear and trepidation over accusations of insensitivity to her narcissistic narratives about relentless (and undiagnosed) health problems. It would seem, unfortunately, that female relational aggression continues up to—and perhaps beyond—the grave.

Critiquing another woman's caregiving style in the later years is akin to putting down parenting skills at a younger age. Both strike at the heart of what most women consider a female legacy: the ability to nurture and mother others.

Women's Words of Wisdom

In this intriguing exploration of how women view in-laws, mutual misunderstandings are all too often the fuel for criticism and judgment of other women. While many women offered positive tributes to their in-laws, we may be part of a larger system that reinforces a special type of aggression between female in-laws. When one person is placed in a subservient or dependent position by virtue of marriage and feels unable to respond genuinely to others, negative emotions can escalate to fury. As suggested, taking care of yourself and surrounding yourself with people who love and affirm you can be powerful antidotes, as can letting go of grudges and advice giving.

In caregiving situations, a continuum of aggressive behaviors both overt and covert can spring up as women feel their efforts unappreciated and their abilities questioned. The best approach to defusing conflict in these cases is having a guiding principle of "What is best for the older woman?" As with other aggressive exchanges, even well-intended words can be inflammatory when they hold the potential to be interpreted as judgment or criticism.

CHAPTER 10

Mrs. Popularity and the Mom Clique

I just don't know how you do it all!

—AN AT-HOME MOTHER TO A FULL-TIME FEMALE EXECUTIVE

What she's really saying is, "You selfish person, you're neglecting your children and home."

—THE FEMALE EXECUTIVE

Even something as simple as reproduction has implications for RA, because fertility, birth control, and childbearing all require a delicate balance between self-sufficiency and connection with others. Once a woman has children, she tends to make career choices that accommodate others (children and spouse), often accepting jobs that are lower paying but more flexible, again reinforcing the primacy of relationships for women. Children, day care, schooling, and extracurricular activities also challenge women to succeed in a whole other arena: mothering. Often, the entrée to many of the motherhood circles in which issues related to children are managed (for example, sports teams, Girl Scouts, and the PTA) can be blocked by another woman in a covert form of the same RA already described.

Drawing the Lines

Deb, an accomplished physician and mother of two, observed that women separate themselves into those who are outside the home and in career settings and those who are working within the home. These two groups are often at odds and even critical of each other regarding children and child rearing. Deb says, "The message is that if you are a professional woman employed outside of the home, you are not tending to your family or the community needs in the same way that those moms who stay at home do."

In the following pieces, women speak about the aggression that can occur between women in the home or community setting.

Women of 2000, More Stressed Than Ever Before!

GAIL FONDA

A couple invited us over for Shabbat dinner where they performed an elaborate ceremony with their very sweet young daughters, reading Hebrew to each other and reciting prayers. The meal was superb, and after the dinner, it was suggested that the women sit at the kitchen table and talk a while. It's been a *long* time since I've taken time to sit and talk with women.

One wife began talking of her husband being a male chauvinist, because they already have four children and he wants another. She works part-time three mornings a week to get away from the children. She doesn't want another child, and her husband doesn't even want her to work part-time! Does she have it all?

Our hostess is a full-time homemaker, but she does help her husband with his at-home software business, which gives her plenty of time to cook and help the girls with their schoolwork. Another of the guests was also an at-home mother who blatantly asked me why I work full-time. I was shocked to hear that question, but said we need the money and health insurance that my job provides.

She rudely asked why my husband didn't take care of that. I told her the truth, which is that my husband thinks it should be fifty-fifty between men and women, and that I should contribute half of the household expenses and work. That simply isn't possible, because I don't make very much money even though I work full-time.

When the talk turned to children, the same woman asked me why we don't adopt. I don't have any children, and I am too old to have them now. Is it really her business?

I think a lot of women do *have it all*, but I just don't know any of them! Women of 2000 are the same as the women of 1900! How insulting for women to criticize other women for not living their lives in the same fashion. Why do I have to follow the leader?

Several women echoed Gail's perception of both subtle and overt criticism from other women if they were childless, either by choice or chance. Some expressed feelings of being blamed for infertility when they deliberately delayed pregnancy for career or other reasons. "It was like other women felt I deserved to have problems, since I didn't have kids right away like they did," said one mother who had a difficult time conceiving in her mid-thirties.

The next story shows another side of motherhood aggression.

Sugar and Spite

ANONYMOUS IN PENNSYLVANIA

I feel very strongly that relational aggression is very prevalent among adult women. I have personally experienced and witnessed bullying in the Parent Teacher Organization.

In my children's school is a woman who volunteered her time within the PTO in various aspects. She was friends with another woman, who had been asked to step down due to conflicts she created. These two women in turn looked for anything to complain about regarding the participation of others in the PTO. They talked behind people's backs. They complained about how others were running programs. They would not call parents who had volunteered to help with the programs they were chairing, claiming they didn't need any help. The rest of the board disagreed with this perspective, but they continued to bring up the PTO bylaws and rules and regulations, creating tension and lengthy meetings. They spoke to some people and snubbed others.

The Kid Game

Key differences that emerged with adult RA were shifts in the way roles were played out, and the targets of aggression. While teens lob verbal grenades directly at each other, mothers sometimes find their children pulled into the Queen Bee's "sting zone." This indirect aggression may take on a milder form as one-upmanship between moms or become more virulent with an all-out attack on a child.

Thirty-year-old Sharon reflects back on her years as a new mother and her closeness with other women, regardless of their work arrangements. "I have never felt as supported as I did then. There was this circle of women that went through Lamaze classes together, then we did 'Moms Morning Out,' then baby playdates, and it was wonderful, the way it should always be. But somehow, the circle fell apart, and the women got back into that competitive mode again, only using children as a way to one-up each other."

Using children as a way to position oneself as superior to other women is a dynamic most of us have observed, if not participated in. The competition-by-virtue-of-children goes something like this, according to an e-mail I received from Gwen, the mom of two teenaged girls: "My daughter is going to XYZ Ivy League college." "My daughter found the perfect size 2 prom gown . . . and it was only $400!" "My son is valedictorian of his class." and so on.

In this game of bidding for status, motherhood and its outcome are one more plus in the struggle to establish superiority. A woman psychiatrist commented on the tendency of mothers to believe they are personally responsible for their children doing well, saying: "In reality, I think it's part genetics, part crap shoot."

Sometimes, women aggress directly through their children, as this poem suggests.

Unsportswomanlike Behavior

CATHIE JACOBSON

> When sitting at a ball game full of support and wit,
> I witness a bad pitch and a competitor is hit . . .
>
> My heart goes out to the unfortunate child,
> But it's part of the game and some pitches go wild.
>
> My son is the catcher behind the plate,
> And there's someone behind him yelling in rage.
>
> She's accusing my boy of conspiring to hurt,
> Her son, who was batting and is now in the dirt.

She bullies and yells—she's out of her mind,
You'd think this 10-year-old had committed a crime!

She rants and she raves and continues to vent,
"They planned this," she says. "This was done with intent!"

As her hysteria continues towards my son and others,
Another pipes up—her 75-year-old mother!

A teenage ump is overseeing the game,
A child himself—these two he can't tame!

My son looks at me with tears in his eyes,
He knows he did nothing to earn their despise.

So without even thinking I hop out of the bleachers,
With rage in my eyes, I've a lesson to teach her . . .

She's made my son cry with her incessant yelling,
And the anger in me is seething and swelling.

By the time I arrive, I'm full of fury,
I'm now the bully and she needs to be worried.

We exchange words as if from the mouth of a sailor,
Then I raise my fist, I'm certain to nail her.

I soon hear the voices of the ump and our coach,
Only then did I cease and ease up my approach.

I never hit her, only words were exchanged,
But the damage was done, a war had been waged.

I'd sunk to her level, I was no better than she,
Usually spunky and fun, now the bully was me!

What an interesting sight we must have been,
Caught in a situation where no one could win.

All of the years of sportsmanship teaching I'd done,
Was now out the window—my pride—there was none.

As I try to reconcile my behavior that day,
I certainly could have handled things another way.

But my maternal defenses had conquered my brain,
And I became another statistic at a little league game.

The chain of bullying began with one mother
And not too long after, it ended with another.

In the adult years, RA can take on yet another twist when hurt-ful behaviors are also played out through children, inflicting twice the harm. Several women described this form of bullying, which extends mom-to-mom aggression one step further. Sometimes a Queen Bee sets the stage for the hapless son or daughter of her victim to be left out at school or sports. Exclusion from sleepovers and birthday parties, befriending or not befriending targeted chil-dren, and spreading rumors that involve multiple family members are all examples of double-damage RA.

Doreen, the mother of a six-year-old girl, told me of a situa-tion where one of her friends suggested, "Tell your daughter not to associate with Amanda [another six-year-old who lived in the neighborhood]. Her mom is a real bitch."

Life with children expands and constricts a woman's world in ways that seem more dramatic than for men. For a relationship-conscious woman, the type and number of connections she makes after motherhood are of a different quality than those from her single days. Children and parenting practices, too, bring a vul-nerability that is the inherent Achilles' heel of mothers. When a child is drawn in and/or targeted because of a conflict between a Queen Bee and the child's mother, a different kind of victimiza-tion occurs. Consider the following stories from women who wit-nessed the spillover effect of aggression.

Camp Cruel
RHEA

One summer, I took a job in another state as nurse at a sum-mer camp for wealthy boys and girls. Because I worked there, my children were also allowed to attend, an opportunity they never would have been given otherwise. It turned out that Bonnie, the activities director, was a woman my age, also with two children who were attending camp. She and I ended up sharing a cabin, since we were required to be the two adults on-site at all times.

At first, things went pretty well, and I was relieved to have Bonnie there. She seemed a lot like me, and our children were the same age. She lived close by and knew a lot about the area, but really disliked being confined to camp. Somehow, something went wrong, but I'm not sure what. Bonnie had an argument with the camp director and then found out I was making more money than her. She turned on me for no reason, ignoring me when I was in our room and making comments about how difficult camp was on the phone so I could hear.

I tried to stay out of whatever problems Bonnie was having and do my job, but one day my younger daughter, Ashley, came to my cabin crying and saying she was being moved. It turned out Bonnie told the camp director that a mother of one of Ashley's cabinmates had called and complained about her. According to Bonnie, the mother wanted Ashley moved immediately, so the camp director did it. Of course, Ashley was terribly upset, because she thought the girls in her cabin were friends and none of them had acted like there were any problems. After things settled down, I asked the cabin counselor, who I knew pretty well, whether there had been anything negative about Ashley. She said no, which convinced me that Bonnie made up the complaint, but there was no way to prove it.

Bonnie made a point of being supersweet to the camp director, who often came to me for advice on campers who were sick or not doing well. Bonnie would huddle with this woman and look at me as if I was the subject of discussion, and would walk away whenever I came up to the two of them. I guess she asked for different accommodations, because she got moved to another cabin not long after the Ashley incident.

To this day, it hurts me to think that Bonnie might have used Ashley to act on her feelings toward me. I know she was unhappy at the camp, and that she didn't like the director, but the way she handled it all was immature and cruel. I'm sure Ashley has forgotten it, but I haven't.

Although the camp nurse situation was one that arose out of chance circumstances, even longstanding friendships can be dissolved by maternal RA.

A Toxic Friend and Mother

MICHELLE SMITH

My best friend of twelve years is no longer a friend—or someone I ever want to see again. We had a huge falling-out, in which she reverted to adolescent behavior and cussed me up one side and down the other, leaving me in a heap of tears and guilt. How does that happen? In my case, I think I recognized, but failed to acknowledge, qualities in her that made her very difficult to be around. Having been friends with her since high school, I had no other concept of what friendship was all about.

Over time, we married and had children. I observed her treatment of other people and grew increasingly discouraged and annoyed. However, until her child, then a toddler, started bullying *my* toddler (a very passive kid), I never thought to take a stand on the way she treated me. As a mother (and a momma-bear, I admit) my priorities changed, and I no longer wanted to be around her. I freely admit to making my share of obvious and stupid mistakes in provoking her behavior toward me, but given our history as friends and my short-sightedness at the thought that it was actually *her* I didn't want to be around, not her kid, I failed to communicate appropriately. I managed to provoke her in a way that I never, ever thought her capable of. She was so hostile to me that I feared for my safety and that of my children. What is strange is that I did not say anything to her that I would not have felt free to say to the people that I now consider my true friends. She just took everything so incredibly personal and twisted it in a way that was not normal.

I've been through a tremendous amount of guilt, pain, and growth since our break-up, but do not regret what has happened, as I have learned so much. I wish I could warn others and save them the heartache, even though I appreciate my own growth as a result of the situation.

The following story is another variation on how maternal RA can wound. The hurt sustained by questions about her mothering abilities stayed with this woman for a longer time than many others.

The Mom Attack

JOYCE GILLIES VISCOMI

When my husband and I had our first fight, I cried for hours afterward, while he sat complacently watching TV. "How can he be so insensitive?" I wondered. His reaction to the fight made it clear that there is a major difference in how men and women perceive arguments: men get over it; women tend to dwell on the issue.

I have discovered that the major conflicts that have arisen in my life relate to my children. I can become as defensive as a mother bear defending her cubs; no issue can bring out the aggressiveness in women faster than the issue of child rearing. Since everyone's life experiences are diverse, unique perspectives on the right way to raise a child collide often with other women's viewpoints. It starts when the children are still in the hospital nursery, when we compare the weights and heights of our offspring, and it does not improve with age. While I tend to choose my friends carefully to avoid this type of confrontation, that does not mean we have not had our differences.

Recently, I had a conflict with one of my closest friends about teenage issues—boyfriends, disrespectful language, and what constituted appropriate movies. Later, at my house, my friend was visibly horrified as my daughter and all of her friends (two girls and one boy) went upstairs to our computer room, because we were getting ready to have a prayer group meeting downstairs. As soon as I realized what had happened, I sent the kids downstairs to our basement to do homework. We have house rules about this—no one of the opposite sex near the bedrooms. Nonetheless, my friend grew even more upset and shrieked, "Aren't you going to check on the kids? Answer me! Answer me now!"

Wow! I never knew she had the capacity to go ballistic like this, so I did what I usually do in situations where someone has been yelling at me; I went outside for a breath of fresh air and tried not to cry. I did, in fact, begin to cry, because I could not understand what had come over my friend. Didn't she trust me? What did she think I normally did when I had kids over at my house? And how many years have we known each other?

I realize now that some of this was a power struggle with an objective to prove that each of us was a "good mother."

Though our philosophical views on raising children became abundantly clear on this one night, both of us were seeking affirmation that our efforts to raise daughters who could manage to stay out of trouble was going to be the proof that we were good mothers. My approach—leaving some decisions up to my daughter, whom I trust will use good judgment most of the time—directly flew in her face as a traditional mother with a more authoritarian code of ethics.

My friend and I managed to work this one out, crying on each other's shoulders for an hour after this outburst, which proved to be cathartic, but still, I know I will never be able to look at her in the same way again, and I know she will never see me the same way either. Having bared our souls for that particular moment might have been a good thing, but I guarantee that in the future, I will probably be much more careful about the things I confide to her about my child.

When children are either the impetus for or the target of another woman's RA, mothers experience pain for both themselves and their sons or daughters. Sometimes, women who might not have the courage to step out of the victim role on their own behalf do so when their child is involved. At other times, moms inadvertently present the wrong role model response to RA by lashing out with anger or retreating into passivity.

Women's Words of Wisdom

Cliques and manipulation, stereotyped as adolescent activities, are alive and well in community groups such as the PTA and booster club where women predominate. Once again, the issue of power is mentioned as a catalyst, with the suggestion that engaging in such behaviors may be motivated by a need to dominate or elevate oneself.

When children become unwitting pawns in the aggression-power game, not only are their mothers hurt deeply, but a code of behavior is modeled that will ultimately damage sons and daughters. Any woman who reads the stories in this chapter will better understand the need to be careful when involving children in relationships with other women—whether by bragging about them or exposing them to direct aggression from a toxic person. Mothering skills and style can provide particularly potent ammunition against another woman. Tolerance for differences in parenting style, as well as compassion for whatever problems may arise in the course of raising a family, would go a long way toward eliminating relational aggression.

As the women respondents suggest, there needs to be a recognition that the life of a mother is rarely without challenges, and those who are deliberately or accidentally childless should not be judged and belittled. Feeling you are inadequate as a friend, classmate, coworker, or acquaintance is traumatic, but having your mothering or childbearing skills questioned strikes at a completely different and more vulnerable place.

CHAPTER 11

Relational Aggression Where You Least Expect It

I was always the type who had a very small group of female friends. You know, where I come from, the streets of Baltimore, you had to kick the next chick out of the box, 'cause the game was tight.

—JADA PINKETT SMITH, ACTRESS

Whether ethnicity influences relational aggression is a question I am asked frequently. Before and after *Girl Wars* was published, I heard from many readers and contributors who had strong feelings about the subject, and to this day the most animated and interesting discussions during my workshops and lectures are often about this topic. In my work with adolescent girls, I have had the opportunity to collaborate with a diverse group of young and adult women, many of whom have shared their opinions about race and relational aggression. Since I believe the topic is an important one for all women, I decided to further explore the nuances of inter- and intraracial RA.

You Just Don't Understand

In the middle of a session of one of the programs I direct for adolescent girls, a woman I admire and respect approached me.

"What makes you think you can work with African American girls?" she asked. "You have no idea what it's like to be black." I was stunned and so busy dealing with the crowd of young women that I didn't know how to answer her, but I couldn't shake a feeling of concern.

Later, she and I discussed her comment. My belief had always been that exposure to women from different backgrounds enriched any program in which adolescents or adults were involved. She reiterated that it was impossible for me to work effectively with young women of color, because I would never be able to really appreciate how they felt.

Obviously, she was right on one point—I will never know what it's like to be an African American teen. At the same time, I wondered what message would be given if only women with identical skin colors and backgrounds were allowed to participate in a program on positive relationship skills. She was firm in her beliefs. We ended the conversation by agreeing to disagree, and to this day I appreciate her honesty and consider her a talented colleague.

The ability of *all* women to share intuitively certain understandings and experiences is a topic with which many women wrestle. As the following story shows, even women from the same ethnic backgrounds can still experience such failure to communicate that they engage in RA.

Sister Support . . . Or Not
ANONYMOUS

Three years ago, I was asked to join a number of senior administrators at breakfast meetings on the topic of equity. I was informed that since I had written my dissertation on topics associated with this initiative, my insights were needed. As an indigenous woman, I was suspicious about the roles that the committee members would predetermine for me based on gender and ethnicity. Too often, I've learned that administrators invite me to participate in the hope that I will speak to a women's or ethnic perspective only. I was also concerned because there are few indigenous women on our faculty or even on our campus. The choice of inviting me to be on the committee might put some noses out of joint, which, in fact, happened. The first instances were the gossip about my affiliation as a graduate student amongst the ranks of more established scholars and administrators. Then there was the shunning, followed by an intensive letter-writing campaign by a couple of "voiced" indigenous women, who felt that since they had tenure and/or many more years of experience than myself, they should be on the committee and not me. I learned from those experiences that while I had naively assumed that I would find collegiality and a sense of sisterhood among the other indigenous women, what I found was competition and bullying. At this point, I have little to do with these women and even polite greetings have deteriorated to no contact at all. My fear is that as I am considered for tenure-track positions on this campus, these women may once again raise their voices to insure that my inclusion in the workplace is limited.

When women from particular backgrounds are invited to participate in activities for the very reason of making the population diverse, RA can still arise, prompted by resentment and competition. Irrational as it may seem, some women don't support programs that mix the ethnicities, ages, or life situations of women to be successful, and may even invest their energies in overt sabotage. Tracy, a health care provider, described her struggles to launch a multiethnic task force, and told me she ultimately failed because of bickering between the women involved. "Each person felt their priorities were the most important ones, and that no one else understood the needs of their particular ethnic group."

A white woman who grew up in a diverse neighborhood remarked on the divide she sees between blacks and whites now that she is an adult residing in Texas. "Our neighborhood is half black and half white, very middle-class, not the neighborhood of yesterday, but women segregate themselves anyway, black with black and white with white. I grew up in a very different background, with a single mom, living in the worst of neighborhoods, and being bused to a black school. I would be comfortable now with friendships from both white and black women, but that hasn't happened—my attempts to get together haven't been returned. The black women stick with their black friends."

Latina Perspectives

M. García, a Latina in her early twenties, is a coordinator of youth programs.

I have noticed a great deal of put-downs amongst people who look like each other. There's more aggression *within* ethnic groups than between ethnic groups. The more one succeeds, the more the others become resentful. With me, my peers were critical because of what I have accomplished. Even my family members have thought that I perceive myself as better than them. However, in other ways, once a person reaches this stage in life and she has done something that is not within the ethnic (cultural) boundaries, then she does become somewhat of an outsider.

In regards to other groups, such as white women, it's not as aggressive. The sad thing about it is that Mexican women always excuse the behavior of white women, because they are "ignorant" or "naïve."

Aggression may occur because of mere tension. Within some cultural/ethnic groups, openly discussing these issues is not welcome. That can, in itself, lead to aggression against each other and victimization of each other. A Mexican woman can look at another Mexican woman and ask herself, What is so special about her? What about me? and so on. Nevertheless, the fact that women do not express those feelings within their circles can lead to aggressive behavior.

For Ms. Garcia, RA comes from both other Latina women, who resent her success, and white women, who don't understand her.

Another woman agrees that the RA from those more like you ethnically can be somewhat harder to take. Eva is an older Mexican American woman with extensive experience in human services, contract compensation, and affirmative action. Currently, she helps to run a leadership program for young Latinas. Eva first offers her thoughts on RA in adult women.

Women aren't more aggressive than girls. In the work environment, adult women experience jealousy going up the career ladder. I was the first female to do so, but I didn't encounter much hostility from other women. I believe hostility results from a sense of weakness and inferiority—when the aggressor feels inferior, she will attempt to improve her self-worth by downplaying the worth of others. Typically, the victim will be someone perceived as weaker than the aggressor, which will most likely be a sure thing.

Aggression is more intense within the ethnic group because it is familiar. Women don't tend to be as aggressive toward something they are unfamiliar with. It is also assumed that light-skinned Latinas have no problems with racial issues and barriers, but sometimes they have just as many problems as the dark-skinned Latinas, which is even more troublesome when they can't even turn to their own ethnic group for understanding.

It is important to teach young women to be strong, responsible, and comfortable with themselves. More sports orientations for young women is a good step, because sports encourage team efforts and structured environments. Also, leadership development is pivotal at all levels for women. Women must be able to start helping girls develop, at least in middle school. Girls need to know that working hard will allow them to gain that edge they need to succeed, and that they should look to themselves for confidence before seeking partners.

Luz is a middle-aged Puerto Rican. She works as an executive in the Northeast and agrees that aggression is an adult phenomenon that takes on a new twist with ethnicity. She says that while teens may be passive, aggression is full-blown in adults. It's present with insecurity in women who are easily threatened, protecting an image, or uncomfortable professionally (even when they are the most competent women around). Luz elaborated on her thoughts:

Hispanic women are less aggressive in general and are nonaggressive in work environments. They are much more aggressive in personal matters, such as jealousy about a significant other. Hispanics defer more, but there can be a catfight when it comes to husbands and other women.

A Latina woman in the United States tends to be less educated and less powerful. She tends to be less aggressive to a white woman than to another Hispanic woman she knows well.

I think in the African American culture, the opposite is true. Hispanics tend to feel *do not* mess with an African American woman. African Americans are worse toward white woman, but they're more open to Latinas. Once you're known to be a minority, the clique opens and you're one of them, just like adolescent cliques.

Aggression is a function of relationships. If children grow up in aggressive environments, they feel that's normal. It's a learned behavior. In aggressive environments, people either rise to aggression or they wither. Aggression may occur via oppression. If people are oppressed, living in unjust, inequitable environments, they get aggressive.

All cultures/genders have different tolerances for aggression. Latina family culture tends to be more passive. Gentleness, kindness, and compassion are the highest values.

The opinions of these women echo thoughts on RA that I've heard from younger women; that is, ethnicity becomes a criteria for inclusion or exclusion in a clique, as well as a source of identity and acceptance. In adult women, a different dynamic seems to occur, with women more likely to use hurtful behaviors on others who share their ethnic identity.

Black Perspectives

Cheena is a middle-aged African American woman who works as an executive director in state government. She shares her thoughts about aggression.

This is difficult to express, but there is definitely aggression among women worldwide. The behavior continues through adulthood, but it's not as intense as it is with younger girls— everything is less intense as you get older. There is definitely jealously, and it's all around. It's within and outside my racial group, but it is different between members of my ethnicity and among women of different ethnicities. In particular, aggression is present with women in supervisory positions.

There is more aggression apparent within the same race. It may be cultural, but it is also the nature of the beast. Primarily, aggression results from feelings of inadequacy. Some women are like that, but it doesn't have to be that way. It depends on the person's upbringing, values, and expectations. If a person finds that aggression works, they will continue to use it.

Sue, a sixty-year-old African American woman who founded a national organization for black women, recognizes that she often has been an aggressor in the work environment, largely as a way to accomplish particular goals.

There is typically an unspoken camaraderie among black women that isn't present among white women or across the color barrier, and black women are most likely to be supportive of each other, depending, of course, on the situation and the individual. Among black women, the touchiest subject is a black man. Because so many are incarcerated in this country, the pickings are slim, so there is a definite aggression between African American women over men. However, the aggression is twofold toward white women who go after black men.

Aggression by black women is definitely strongest toward whites. When economics and the workforce have white and black women working side by side, everything is fine, but when an opportunity doesn't exist for both equally, as perceived by these women, aggression occurs. There's unspoken sisterhood among black women.

Many white women still act superior, which is a behavior that hasn't been eradicated since the times of plantations and slavery, and aggression will exist until there are more women to teach each other about their respective opportunities, cultures, and individualities. White women don't see things from the perspective of black women because they don't share the same experiences. I walk into a room as a woman (my perception), but I am seen by others as a black woman—it is this thought process that needs to change. There is aggression toward white women because they are greeted with more and better opportunities. Black women usually support each other because they have shared similar experiences. There is a dividing line between whites and blacks that can't yet be crossed.

The earning power of women in America compared to men, based on the education and opportunities available is seventy-six cents for white women, sixty-two cents for African American women, fifty-four cents for Latinas, and so on. So women in general have the lack of equality, but white women still don't tend to acknowledge that they still have it better than women of other ethnic backgrounds.

Aggression results from jealousy and a perception of power and influence. Women are astute. When they see power and influence in a woman, they become jealous, which results in aggression, in the traditional sense.

Gayle, a middle-aged African American woman who owns a business that focuses on women's issues, holds a slightly different opinion, although she agrees that within-group hostility and competition is greater than between groups.

There is historically within the African American community a lot of backbiting. I see it as "The Crab Syndrome," where you have all these crabs in one pot. Because traditionally there haven't been enough opportunities, people who got the opportunities were resented, because they didn't share. The theory is that there is an attempt to keep African American people at each other for various reasons. Everyone tends to feel threatened. Someone gets something you don't, and you feel threatened. Women who don't feel good about themselves tend to do those types of things.

The best action to take is to get better in touch with yourself. Find out what is important to you. Find the opportunity to get those needs satisfied. Conflict is about not getting a need satisfied. Someone is either feeling not valued, not affirmed, or not taken seriously. Until you get comfortable with yourself, then communicate that and talk about what's going on, you're not going to establish healthy relationships with others. They're not mind readers, they need to know. Work with people to see what can happen.

In the News

In October 2002, *Essence* magazine published an article titled "White Women at Work." Seven black female executives were invited to discuss their observations about white women in the workplace and to describe specific conflicts and challenges they had experienced. The gist of their discussion was that white women were no longer allies in the fight for equal opportunity and sometimes even acted in aggressive ways, betraying and back-stabbing black women for the sake of professional gain.

In March 2003, a second article ran on the topic of relationships between black and white women; this time a discussion between several white businesswomen provided the subject matter. These women readily acknowledged that inequities are still faced by black women in the workplace, but they also pointed to the wealth of programs promoting specific opportunities for women of color, which created a reverse discrimination and led to negative feelings. The white women described a tentativeness in their relationships with black women, in part because they had been on the receiving end of somewhat hostile interactions.

In summary, each article generated an "action plan" that could improve relationships. Black women's suggestions for overcoming differences were:

- Study the cultural climate at the workplace and use this information to come up with strategies.
- Realize that you might need to prove yourself by making an extra effort and working harder than everyone else.
- Network.
- Educate white women about ethnic identities.
- Create positive relationships with white women.
- Be proactive.
- Put together a group for women of color in the workplace.

White women's suggestions for creating greater unity included:

- Encourage more open dialogue about concerns and issues between black and white women.
- Build nonexclusive networks.
- Cross-mentor between women of all ethnicities.
- Draw on humor and recognition of similarities as well as differences to promote better relationships.

There's a Place for Us

As with women of similar ethnicities, it would seem that women from the same faith traditions should be able to set aside aggressive tendencies and take shelter in relationships with each other. Several stories I received and discussions with religious leaders suggest that, sadly enough, this is not the case. Even within religious communities, RA can fracture relationships and cause discord for both men and women

Holy No
SANDRA H.

I guess you could say I'm sort of a religious drifter. I had tried churches of several different denominations in our community, but never settled on one. Then my family and I started attending a large, fundamentalist church I'll call the House of God.

Initially, we felt very welcome there. Everyone greeted us like we were old friends and invited us to come back. I began taking my two elementary school children to some of the activities for kids, where other moms would be, too. Every time we went, I made an effort to be nice to the women, but after a few pleasantries, they would turn back to each other and shut me out.

I couldn't believe a place that claimed to spread love around could be so shallow! My kids liked going there, so I tried harder, attending some special services for women and volunteering to help distribute Thanksgiving food baskets. Again and again, it was the same story. Just like high school, the House of God had its own little clique, too. The inner circle of women clustered around the pastor's wife as if she were the homecoming queen of years gone by. I got the impression that I wasn't religious enough, or good enough, to be part of their crowd. We stopped going to church there, but later on I met another woman who had the same experience. From time to time, I see women I knew from the House of God at the mall or in the grocery store, and they walk by me as if I don't exist. I guess I really never did—for them.

There are few—if any—sacrosanct places when it comes to RA. Wherever women gather, it seems to happen. One pastor noted with frustration that certain female members of her congregation acted in ways that were remarkably hurtful to others. There was even a time when she was almost the victim of a Queen Bee assault.

> I think it is an issue to do with power in congregations, or that's the way I perceived it at the time. It was a very small congregation that I grew from about fifty to about two hundred members. That was a lot. When I came there, I was aware that there were particular women who were the so-called leaders in the congregation. They were the ones who did the flowers and did the children and did this and did that and whatever. When the church began to grow, we got a lot of younger couples in, and I think the women who had been there before felt threatened by newcomers. If there was verbal sabotage, I didn't hear that as much as action sabotage, meaning, "I'm not going to let Jan or Terry be involved, you know, they are not ready yet to do Sunday School," or be on a committee, or whatever. So we would work through that. That was woman to woman, never the men saying this about women.
>
> It was amazing, in a church, to see certain women kept on the outside by the others in power. People were graciously polite to them when they met them, but they would talk about them later in their own group. I knew they were never "in," because they were never given positions of power, ever. So it was a relational aggressiveness played out in terms of church committee and structure and maintaining the power structure. I can remember one lady who I will call Joan, who was a really outspoken, aggressive lady, which only escalated during my time at the church. She wasn't afraid to take charge: "I will do this" and "I think we should have done it this way" and "Next time I will do this" and you could see relational withdraw on the part of all the women who interacted with her. I know there were occasions at committees that they could be downright bitchy about Joan.
>
> When I became the target in a play for power by the "in" group, it upset me as much as anything in my career. I even hit the table and had words with them over it. Later, we talked it out one-on-one, but it was disturbing. I didn't want to be spending my time on those kinds of issues.

Women have the attitude that when someone invades our turf we go to war, and, because in a congregation we are not allowed to pull out our guns and grenades, the way the war is fought is by clinging tighter to our own particular power. Then we engage in backbiting or subtle maneuvers to put the person on the outside and make sure she knows she's on the outside.

This woman was struck by the difference in how men and women in the congregation responded differently to the changes she made. While men welcomed newcomers, women felt threatened.

As a leader of programs for adolescent girls, I am often asked if RA is less of a problem in an all-female religious environment. I've discovered that the private school experience can be a breeding ground for aggression—especially when girls live together. In the following story, a woman shares an experience that illustrates that this dynamic persists into adulthood.

Relational Aggression: I Hated Shedding Tears
CARMEN LARKIN

I learned the subtle art of relational aggression in the best proving ground of all: an all-girls' boarding school. Behind the pretty manners and the old Latin prayers was the power struggle to control the playground, what we did for recreation, and who walked next to the sister in charge. It was a fine ballet of alliances and intricate maneuvering for territory and friends. I learned early to observe.

In high school, where I began the journey to becoming a nun, the sisters ran a program for young ladies who thought they might have a religious vocation. Nine of us from different schools came together to live basically as nuns. Custom and tradition was that the first girl to enter the convent on Entrance Day was considered the "oldest" or senior postulant of that group. When it came time to move onto the novitiate, we knew the same custom would apply. I arrived at noon, number one, staking my territory for the girls from my school. Relational aggression, subtle, at its best.

There was another contender for number one from our sister school, and she was Machiavellian in return. In the convent, there is, once a month, a practice called Chapter of Faults, in which you confess your transgressions against the rules of the community and your fellow sisters. After I went and knelt before Mother Mistress and confessed my sins, the contender stood up and accused me of a "particular friendship" with a postulant. You can't defend yourself or speak about it ever, so I kissed feet for setting a bad example. Check and checkmate! But I was still number one. Relational aggression, I know your name and face; I live and breathe you every day.

Sarah is a middle-aged rabbi who does not currently lead a congregation. She talks about her career in terms of working with women and confronting RA.

When I became a student rabbi I was twenty-six or twenty-seven and the women in my mother's generation had a hard time accepting me, because there weren't other female rabbis. Part of it was they didn't have the chance I had and they were jealous. They would do things like call the president and lodge silly complaints about me, things like my lipstick color.

The majority of my congregation was closer to my age and very supportive. The women were very receptive and nonjudgmental. My being female was very freeing for many of them and for me, too. I devoted myself ninety hours a week to the congregation and worked very hard with teenagers. I had confirmation classes, ninth and tenth graders, where there was potential for girls to be snotty to each other. One of the things I said from the beginning was you can't be judgmental. You will have to leave meanness outside the door. Within that class, all the girls learned to be supportive of one another.

At one point, some people asked me how I could stand it there (at the synagogue) and I asked what they were talking about. They were referring to the women being so catty, but honestly, I hadn't seen it.

Even now in the women's groups, there is someone I work with who is very difficult, one of those people whose insecurities lead her to be rather rigid. Honestly, there is nothing we can do about it but pray. People have tried to talk to her, but she is in a place where she can't hear what they have to say. At the end of one group, someone was ready to start on a riff about this woman, and I said, "No, accept the things we cannot change. There is nothing we can do to make this person any different, so it's not worth our time to sit and complain about the person."

I certainly will say that Jewish women can be just as nasty as the rest of the universe. In the synagogues there are always women's groups who are indeed very supportive of each other and the congregation. I've done Jewish federation work, and I've known women in sororities, and trust me, they can be as catty as the next person. I do believe that members of institutions that are primarily social gathering places can tend to be much more aggressive and rigid, with a lot of "shoulds." Having goals and purposes can help avoid some of that crap.

While religious communities and their female infrastructures should be places where women can find a respite from the world of RA, so common at work, home, and play, the same power struggles and residual insecurities that create Queen Bees, Middle Bees, and Afraid-to-Bees elsewhere can turn sanctuaries and synagogues into places of hurt and betrayal.

Women's Words of Wisdom

Based on the interviews and stories used in this chapter, RA does not discriminate, presenting serious issues for women of color, both within and between specific ethnic groups. Minority cliques that keep women affiliated with only those who share their cultural backgrounds or skin colors undermine the ability of all women to have open discussions about differences and similarities. Some of the women who provided input on this subject might argue that even within ethnic groups, those who share certain cultural experiences still do not understand or accept one another. Others go further and suggest minority women may actually use harsher aggressive behavior against those who are most like them physically or culturally.

In the same way, women in religious organizations may not recognize or acknowledge that their behavior is hurtful or aggressive. The Queen Bee organizer who takes charge of church or synagogue events may view herself as helpful rather than domineering. The

Middle Bee who controls the amount of information she shares with or withholds from newcomers can manipulate others. Afraid-to-Bees may be especially intimidated in religious organizations, where expressing conflict can be seen as inappropriate.

Assumptions and stereotypes based on appearance and power can shatter relationships between women. Ethnicity, socioeconomic status, religious beliefs, and education can become artificial barriers that divide women and perpetuate RA. As in other contexts, the absence of open and honest discussions among women can maintain the status quo of animosity and aggression.

The constant of desire for power and status, as well as low self-esteem, underlies much of the aggression women described in this chapter. Themes from the discussions on women in feminist organizations resonate here, with the perception that one woman's success, regardless of her color, is often cause for jealousy and resentment, rather than celebration.

Surprisingly, many of the RA themes expressed by women in relation to ethnicity were echoed by those in religious organizations. First was the trend toward intense aggression within groups, be they of the same faith or ethnic background. Second, a tendency to obtain security by maintaining the current power structure was also common to both groups. Third, in a struggle for individual status, behaviors such as gossip, intimidation, manipulation, and exclusion were used to keep the larger group divided.

Write Therapy

In the cover letters that accompanied many of the stories in part two, the benefit of expressing difficult or unresolved emotions about RA through writing narratives or poetry for this book was stressed again and again. Telling one's story and finding a voice that shared deep hurts with others provided a powerful opportunity to begin healing. Women discovered that working through problematic situations on paper offered a safe opportunity to explore past hurts, and even began the process of problem solving and resolution. In the next part of this book, I will introduce other strategies that can help you overcome RA in your life.

PART THREE

Recognize, Revise, and Internalize

Changing the RA Way of Life

*If I've learned anything after all
these years of being the object
Of your seething-green-eyed-rage
it is that this is your problem
not mine. I have to deal with my
own insecurities, and I'm working on it.
Take me down a notch. But only
in your mind. I will not let you take me down a notch.
No more.*

ALIZA SHERMAN, "TAKE ME DOWN"

CHAPTER 12

Who Are You in the Bee Dynamic?
A Relational Aggression Assessment

Then I realized that what she was doing was relational aggression. It was such a relief to put a name to it.

—A WOMAN IN HER THIRTIES DESCRIBING HER INVOLVEMENT
WITH A QUEEN BEE FRIEND

During the course of a day, each of us encounters people who may interact with us in less-than-respectful ways. Many of them may be women: the cashier who rolls her eyes to others in line when we can't figure out the grocery store's credit card machine, the female boss who fires off an imperative e-mail that sounds like a threatening command rather than a request, or the friend who cuts us short in the middle of a soul-baring conversation. Most of us aren't demoralized by these slights and recognize them as isolated events.

When actions are intensely aggressive, however, and/or the situation is sustained and extreme, or if there has never been movement beyond the middle school mean girl mindset, being involved in *any* form of RA can change the way a woman relates to the world. Grown-up Queen Bees are likely to feel a sense of betrayal, indignation, and threat after aggressive tangles. Mature Middle Bees may feel a range of mild to extreme discomfort depending on their involvement in aggressions or lack thereof. Lifelong Afraid-to-Bees can retreat into victim roles with even slight provocations.

After she was the target of a campaign to spread rumors about her at work, one professional woman, who denied being in a Queen Bee, Middle Bee, or Afraid-to-Bee role, said, "I am by nature an extremely trusting person, and when that trust is betrayed, I am just . . . I am just rattled. It really hurt me." For her, the in-your-face RA was impossible to overcome. After several months, she quit her job.

Another woman shared this account of prolonged abuse from her Queen Bee boss and the process that led her to realize that she was not at fault.

My Boss Was a Bully

BARBARA MOLDAUER

My dream job had become a nightmare. After two years in which I could do no wrong, I received an unsatisfactory performance evaluation so cutting it felt like a physical blow. Just six months before, my boss described me as "creative, thoughtful and sensitive, a strong mentor and an excellent listener." This time she wrote, "Beautiful work products are meaningless if they damage relationships and the team. Take care not to dominate the flow of conversation. Adopt a 'learning behavior.' Stretch the rubber band toward the 'thinking' and 'sensing' dimensions of your personality type."

She watched as I read. "I worked hard on this. Don't rush through it."

"Would you like me to resign?" I asked.

My bewilderment grew when, instead of accepting my resignation, she entreated me to stay. I didn't know what to do. I'd been so eager to work for this woman, I'd taken a salary cut. After a single interview, she offered me my dream job: a management position in the public relations department of a century-old association with a noble purpose and a highly educated membership. A compelling writer and a charismatic speaker, she mesmerized audiences, while I, a professional speechwriter, was terrified to address a group. A cut in salary seemed a small price to pay for the opportunity to learn from her.

After just three months on the job, I received a promotion and a raise. I thought: Finally, a boss who appreciates me! Yet, even as I exulted in my good fortune, I felt an under-current of unease when her deputy abruptly resigned, telling me, "You're the flavor of the month. Watch out—it fades quickly."

I had been there about a year when Jenny, a young writer, went from angel to devil virtually overnight. My boss explained what had happened in her written account of a two-hour counseling session with Jenny.

The problems started when Jenny complained: "I feel like the ball in a ping-pong game. Three people are editing my work. They all want different things, and they all want lots of changes. I feel frustrated and exhausted by the emotionally charged atmosphere. I worry that someone will have a bad day, and I'll get axed."

My boss's response was to conclude that Jenny was tem-peramentally unsuited to the job: "Her Myers-Briggs type (a personality test) likes to receive information in structured and orderly ways and tends to catastrophize."

Jenny resigned the week after the counseling session. I believed my boss when she said it was for the best. After all, my boss prided herself on her people skills, honing them at every opportunity with workshops and self-help books.

Asked to find ways to speed up production of news releases, a team of junior staffers recommended doing away with edit-ing and rewriting. I voiced a concern that quality and produc-tivity would plummet. Angrily, my boss declared that her main concern was team building, not the work product. I held my tongue and did as the team directed, even when my misgivings proved to be well-founded.

Shortly afterward, I received the unsatisfactory review. Deeply wounded by its angry and intensely personal tone, I blamed myself and thought, Maybe I really am obnoxious. When my boss offered to hold a retreat to induce me to stay, I resolved to figure out what I'd done wrong and fix it.

The retreat was a great success. We cried, hugged, shared confidences, and bonded. My boss revealed that her husband had walked out on her while she was still recovering from the hysterectomy she'd had right after Jenny left. I said to myself, That explains it.

I will never forget the moment, barely a month later, when I realized that the camaraderie of the retreat was the false calm of the eye of a storm. I had created a poster my boss liked so much, she was going to unveil it at a black-tie dinner for the board of directors. As I rolled and tied posters with elaborate silver bows, we chatted companionably.

"Everything's going great," I said.

She snarled back, "Why shouldn't it?"

Determined to redeem myself, I labored twelve hours a day, seven days a week, produced prodigious amounts of work, and completed a massive report that had fallen behind schedule. My boss informed me I was still not meeting her expectations and berated me about another woman's work product. When I tried to explain the difficulties I, too, was having with this woman, my boss said angrily, "Take responsibility. Stop blaming!"

Again, I protested that she was being unfair.

"Are you saying you're a victim?" my boss asked, her lip curling in contempt. She ordered me to return to my office and wait. Four hours later, at six o'clock on a Friday, I discovered that she had left earlier without a word. She called in sick all the next week.

Upon her return, she presented me with a second unsatisfactory performance evaluation. The five-inch-thick report I had labored to complete on time was described as "scant." As she stared coldly at me, a small smile playing at the corners of her lips, I saw through the facade of competence to the warped character beneath. Instead of basing her feelings on facts, as emotionally healthy people do, she rewrote reality to justify the rage she felt. When Jenny described the atmosphere in our office as "emotionally charged," I hadn't understood. Now I did, but I wasn't about to resign as she had. Finding a comparable job at my level would be much harder than finding one at Jenny's level. Moreover, I had good reason to believe my boss would not long endure. A senior official had confided to me that she was widely disliked, even despised, for her bullying tactics, mercurial moods, and unbridled fits of rage

I knew the options: I could either appeal to her boss or to human resources. The CEO was a thirty-year veteran who had already announced he was retiring the following year. He rarely came to the office anymore, so that left human resources. The head of HR encouraged me to resign, even as he admitted my boss's real motivation.

"This is personal," he said, explaining that I had no legal recourse because "she's an equal-opportunity abuser."

Christmas that year brought a reorganization that set me up to fail: I was stripped of half my staff, while my responsibilities remained the same. Wondering whether it might be best to resign after all, I made an appointment with the head of HR. Before I could say anything, he told me I was receiving a raise and a generous bonus and then asked, "What can we do to make it right?" Encouraged to believe I could hold on to my job, I said, "Move me." He said he'd do his best, but warned it could take time.

Meanwhile, my boss intensified her efforts to make me so miserable I would quit. I was able to take a long-planned vacation, timed to coincide with my only son's spring break, because the head of HR intervened on my behalf.

Upon my return, I was stunned to learn that I wouldn't be transferred after all. I buried myself in my work, which continued to go well, and noted the toll our standoff had taken on my boss. She had regained the fifty pounds she had lost the previous year and more, and her always erratic attendance had reached the point where she was out more than she was in. I dared to hope that she would resign.

The Friday before Labor Day, I was summoned by an underling in HR who informed me that my job was being eliminated, and I was marched out of the building like a criminal.

At first, I felt the searing pain of a teenager on the outs with the in crowd. Disbelief followed: How could this happen? She was the problem, not me. Then came disillusionment. In the tale "The Emperor's New Clothes," I recalled, an innocent boy shouts the truth and the crowd acknowledges what all can plainly see: their leader is a naked pretender. Ruefully, I thought, Real life isn't like that.

I found it unimaginable that an august institution would allow a bully to carry on unchecked, but carry on she does. Two women were forced out within six months of my departure and more will undoubtedly follow. With the offices on either side of her empty, my boss sits in solitary splendor, her desk turned to the wall to avoid eye contact with passersby.

When your boss is a bully, unethical, or both, staying can be as painful as leaving. Which is the better choice? That's a question each of us can only answer for ourselves.

The other day, I was talking to my fifteen-year-old son about my life these days, much of which revolves around looking for a new job, and about his, much of which revolves around getting the hang of high school social life. Our talk turned to bullies, a subject of concern for both of us. Feeling sorry for myself, I said, "What did I achieve? I was fired anyway."

My son replied, "You stood up to the bully instead of quitting."

My spirits lifted with the pride in his eyes. I thought to myself, "That's what I tell him to do. If I don't set an example, who will?"

If you read this or other stories in this book and find yourself identifying with some of the behaviors or experiences, it might be time to dig deeper and see if you're part of an RA dynamic you haven't recognized. The following questions are designed to help you assess your relational style and may require some soul-searching to come up with honest answers. For each question, select the one behavior that sounds *most* like you.

ATTITUDES

A. Do I believe connections to women at home, work, and play are an important part of my life?

B. Are women often an "end to a means," enabling me indirectly to get things I want for myself?

C. Am I somewhat insecure and afraid of women?

D. Would I choose to be with men rather than women, no matter what the activity?

FRIENDSHIPS

A. Do I have a rich network of female friends?

B. Am I often dissatisfied with the women friends I have?

C. Do I feel my women friends take advantage of me or abuse me?

D. Is there a complete absence of women friends in my life?

Conflict

A. Am I able to resolve disagreements with another woman without hurting her or me?

B. Do I spend a lot of time planning how I will get the best of other women without direct confrontation?

C. Do I give in to other women even when I know I am right?

D. Do I provoke women into conflicts with me, knowing I will do whatever it takes to come out on top?

Relationships

A. Do I respect and cooperate with women, even if they're not individuals I consider friends?

B. Am I only interested in women for what they can do for me or enable me to acquire for myself?

C. Are there any women I know with whom I have positive relationships outside of my friends and family?

D. Do I only choose to interact with women I know I can dominate, manipulate, or humiliate?

Behavior

A. Do I use many types of behaviors in the course of a day, most often relying on assertiveness to interact with others?

B. Am I often the woman who is a contact, passing along what others tell me, staying on top of neighborhood news, and using information to control others?

C. Do I usually allow others to call the shots, rarely speaking up for myself or expressing my true feelings?

D. Am I usually the person "in charge," telling others what to do, making sure my way is everyone's way, and never worrying what others think?

If the A statements describe you best, you sound like a woman who has avoided the "Bee" style of interacting—congratulations! The B choices reflect behaviors common to women in the middle, which can mean participating passively in aggression or doing nothing to stop it. If you related most to the C questions, you may want to take a closer look at the Afraid-to-Bee role and see if it fits you.

It may be hard to face the fact that you relate to any of these RA roles, but perhaps the hardest to admit to are the kinds of behaviors in the D questions—ones that describe a Queen Bee. No woman wants to think of herself as a bully who damages others, but denial is how such aggression becomes internalized. If you've been honest in your answers, you've taken the first and most important step to stopping your hurtful behavior.

Recognizing your role for what it is helps you identify where change needs to occur. Another self-awareness exercise that can promote insight is to think of a typical day in the last week or so, and tally the number of times:

- Another woman chose to collaborate with you on a project
- You were asked to join a group of women in an activity
- A female friend called or wrote just to catch up with you
- Another woman expressed genuine appreciation to you for something you did
- You had a satisfying conversation with another woman in which you both spent an equal amount of time talking
- You gave another woman a sincere compliment
- Another woman made you smile or laugh, or vice versa
- You opted to work with another woman, given the choice of equally qualified males and females

Perhaps your responses to these exercises suggest that you are stuck in a relational pattern that is harmful for you, as well as those around you. Be clear that there is a difference between episodes of RA and a lifestyle in which RA predominates. The woman who is literally unable to shift out of "bee" mode is also likely to be paralyzed emotionally.

Feeling Facts

Another assessment you might want to conduct is a review of how you typically function at home, work, and play, and the emotions you are likely to experience when you are with different people under different circumstances. See if any of the following descriptions sound like you.

Queen Bee Beth is polished, poised, and always prepared, or so it seems. She cruises through her day using behaviors that have been refined over the course of her lifetime to manipulate and control others. Beth never hesitates to use a sharp word or gesture to let other women know how she feels about them. (Men receive only goodwill.) As president of the Junior League, Beth sees her behavior as appropriate—after all, she is in charge. The only time Beth worries about her performance is when she is near Sylvia, a new mother who has natural charm and leadership ability. Beth suspects that Sylvia is establishing her own network of power and will eventually try to take over the presidency, so she works to build herself up by putting Sylvia down.

Beth doesn't think about the many meaningful relationships and opportunities she has lost—or the ones with Sylvia she is steadily sabotaging. No one (including Beth) realizes that underneath, this Queen Bee is anxious, fearful, depressed, and intimidated by other women, particularly those who, like her, seek power. If asked whether she considers herself to be aggressive or a bully, Beth would vigorously deny it, but in reality, the negative persona she projects to the world has corroded her self-esteem, too. It's exhausting and virtually impossible to maintain the kind of control and power Beth wants, because the strategies she uses ultimately damage and drain rather than build and sustain relationships with others.

For Tara, a new college graduate and lifelong Middle Bee, guilt and anxiety are internal responses to everyday interactions that involve either allowing or promoting aggression. In her sorority, she was intimidated by the sisters who were openly aggressive to women outside their circle of friends, but she avoided victimization by occasionally joining in to gossip or ridicule others. Now in her job at a major publishing company, Tara quickly recognizes the same sorority sister behavior from her college days, with one difference: terrified that she won't succeed, Tara seizes the opportunity to undermine the other new hires to her boss, Nancy, who is the quintessential Queen Bee—insecure and hostile to any woman who shows potential.

Tara makes her rounds every morning, gathering information from other young women who view her as friendly. Carefully, she edits facts in the stories she will pass on to Nancy, so as to best position herself as Nancy's favorite new hire. In college, Tara operated from a position of "should or shouldn't have" (as in "I should have spoken up," or "I shouldn't have said or done that"), which was never comfortable. In her role as a malicious Middle Bee, she is so consumed with circulating and regulating information, she misses out on other opportunities to enrich her life and establish genuine connections. She also is setting herself up to be shunned by her peers when they discover her agenda—and they will.

Afraid-to-Bees like Harriet seem to function well, often viewed as the cooperative and hardworking mother, employee, or volunteer. Harriet is one of three single women who share an apartment in the city. At home, Harriet is the housecleaner, grocery shopper, and transportation coordinator by default, still receiving criticism for the way she carries out these tasks. Her job as a sales clerk is disparaged by her roommates, who have managed to find higher paying positions in retail and consider her a failure because she couldn't do the same. Even Harriet's sister-in-law bullies her, calling at the last minute to announce she desperately needs a babysitter for her three unruly children.

Those around Harriet can't see that she resents being a victim, even though she resolutely pastes a smile on her face every morning. Inside, Harriet is full of both anger and doubt: the first in response to continual put-downs by other women and the second because she believes that perhaps she deserves them. Over time, Harriet's failure to respond appropriately to the aggression of other women can lead to negative consequences: depression and even lower self-esteem can be part of a cycle of self-defeating behavior that keeps her trapped as an Afraid-to-Bee.

Aggression as Abuse

As with any trauma, relational aggression is so overwhelming and hard to understand, denial may be a woman's first response. If it's impossible to free herself of the situation, a false belief may evolve that things will improve given enough time or the right circumstances. If this doesn't happen, the wound that results has all the features of abuse: a sense of betrayal, an element of self-doubt and blame, and feelings of hopelessness and anger. While a woman may successfully hide or bury these emotions, the cumulative effects of RA can lead to profound changes in the way she views and relates to others.

For some, this means an inability to trust other women and a heightened sense of vigilance against future threats. For others, pervasive fear prevents the formation of genuine relationships, and a continual grieving process over what might have been is the theme of their lives.

For the Health of It

Sustained RA is traumatic and hurtful to everyone involved, whether as giver, receiver, or witness. Not only will an interaction style saturated with RA poison relationships with others, it can also affect well-being. More than one contributor suggested that hostile Queen Bee types seem to experience a higher than normal incidence of health problems because their energy is so channeled with negativity. It makes sense that frequent and/or intense RA is a stressor with the potential to adversely affect physical and/or emotional health, regardless of the role played.

A study by Australian Health Works showed that workplace bullying created an environment that led to problems such as stress, anxiety, panic attacks, sleep problems, depression, trouble concentrating, and elevated blood pressure. Half of the more than three hundred workers who participated in the study said they had taken sick days to deal with being bullied.

The following stories describe situations where women developed physical and emotional health problems after being involved in sustained RA.

Woman #1: Ann

In my particular situation, I was affected in several ways, including my health. Physically and emotionally, I was a complete wreck. I questioned my skills and abilities. I often sought out reassurance from close friends and family. I found that I was not sleeping at night, but staying awake for hours and getting up to follow the same daily routine. I was a bundle of nerves and my appearance was beginning to be affected. I visited my primary care provider and discovered that my blood pressure also was out of control. In fact, on this visit, my blood pressure was 200/110. I was crying uncontrollably, which was not hard to do when I talked about my situation. Not only was my professional livelihood and my health affected, I was also affected financially.

Woman #2: Jean

I had nightmares, I gained forty pounds, and my blood pressure was the highest it had ever been in my life. I put myself on Zantac because I was experiencing heartburn that was waking me up during the night. I never knew from day to day what my Queen Bee coworker was going to pull next. I dreaded going to work. I started to see a therapist to get help for work-related stress. My coworker, the nurse who tried to help me, also started to see the same therapist as me—the poor therapist got her ears full. It finally escalated to the point that the therapist told me to get out of there.

The first week I left the state my heartburn cleared up and I have been off Zantac since. I have lost forty pounds and my blood pressure is normal. The nightmares lasted about six months after I left.

The Best Cure

For the sake of their health, women who suffer from sustained RA must find ways to free themselves from the destructive dynamic of aggression before it results in serious health consequences. Being motivated to change is just the beginning of a process that can both heal the past and lead to a future of improved mental and physical well-being.

Years of Fears

KATHERINE GERARD

My husband, Ted, and I first met Mary over a decade ago, when Ted accepted a position at a university religious center. Mary was quick to welcome us and was constantly offering to help us get acquainted with the area, so we spent quite a bit of time with her.

Fairly soon, however, I noticed that I often was the butt of Mary's jokes. Ted and I discussed why she apparently thought this behavior was acceptable. He thought it was simply due to the fact that I'm generally pretty good-natured and would not hesitate to joke back, so we let it go. But as time passed, Mary became very public in her criticism. If I mispronounced a word while reading the Old or New Testament lessons, she was quick to point out my mistakes and always in front of others. She began making fun of anything I did, from how I talked, to my driving skills, and my physical appearance and a vision impairment I have.

A year after we arrived, Mary was turning forty, and I asked the office secretary if they were planning anything for her birthday. The secretary explained that she personally had no interest in planning a party, as Mary had been particularly vicious in her comments to her teenage daughter, often reducing the girl to tears.

I agreed to organize a party. A few days before the party, Mary was diagnosed with cancer. Not knowing the prognosis, we worked hard to keep the theme light and away from the usual, "Man, forty is *old*" nonsense. The party was fun and uplifting, but Mary's bullying was about to cost her. Shortly after her cancer surgery, the pastor announced that he was firing her after receiving numerous complaints from choir members, parishioners, and parents about her abusive behavior. However, due to her illness, the personnel committee begged him to reconsider, and he reluctantly agreed to let her work until the end of her contract.

Ted and I pitched in with others to help Mary where we could, taking her for chemotherapy and providing food, financial assistance, and other necessities. Staring at both her mortality and the certain loss of her job, Mary seemed to be reevaluating her approach and, for a while at least, was less abusive.

Once she was deemed cancer free, Mary's old behavior returned with a vengeance. She went through a number of jobs; later I learned it was her constant bullying that was the issue, and I wasn't surprised. But even as I was severing ties with Mary, she was still calling on a regular basis, oblivious to the fact that I didn't respond.

The next incident might again seem trivial, but it, too, caused great distress. A friend repeated a story Mary had told her regarding me. It was silly—Mary claimed that I was such a dangerous driver that when she rode with me, she literally feared for her life. But there was one problem with the story— I had never driven Mary anywhere. My friend went on to say that Mary had told a number of other unflattering stories at my expense, and she was concerned about her behavior.

Another incident occurred involving malicious gossip about Ted. He felt that he could successfully deflect any repercussions from this story without taking legal action. That's one of the differences between him and me. As someone who has dedicated his life to serving God, he manages to find good in anyone. For me, any good that had existed in Mary had long since been lost.

That is the essence of my story, and while there were numerous other incidents, I didn't want to go on too long. Not even therapy served as the kind of catharsis that writing this story did for me, so if nothing else, it was a great exercise in purging some very painful memories. I don't know what you will discover in your research with other women, but I have come to believe that bullies learn to be bullies at home. Those same bullies we encounter on the school playground as children grow up to become even more ferocious. Unless recognized and treated early, this relational dysfunction continues into adulthood, where it negatively affects society as a whole.

How You Score

Understanding RA and its relevance to your life is the beginning of change. Having used the tools in this chapter to assess your RA quotient, you are now aware of whether this dynamic is driving your life in destructive directions. As you examine the different Bee roles and decide which, if any, describes you, the next steps will fall into place.

Whether your relationship patterns match those of a Queen Bee (bully), Middle Bee (in-betweener), or Afraid-to-Bee (victim), the challenge confronting you is to now explore influences from the past that may be driving your actions. Hurtful relational styles do not develop spontaneously, but they will persist if you fail to cleanse yourself of the emotions that fuel them. Through a life review of relationships as well as behavior, you will be able to identify significant people and situations that shaped the way you interact with the women who surround you today.

CHAPTER 13

Healing Residual Relational Aggression
Overcoming the Past

Excessive aggressive or passive behavior comes from the same place of lacking genuine self-worth. The middle ground is to express yourself in kind and loving ways that show your belief in your self-worth."

—DEBRA MANDEL, PSYCHOLOGIST

Throughout life, we tend to be repeatedly attracted to and repulsed by the same kind of individuals. The girl who bullied you in seventh grade was probably a scaled-down version of the choir director who harasses you as an adult. The woman who stands by and watches you be abused by the office manager is not so different from those who crowded around the popular girl in high school and failed to halt her overly aggressive tactics. Identifying traits in women who make you uncomfortable will help both bullies and victims proactively develop a plan for handling challenging peers.

Exploring Past Traumas

The Relationship Timeline is a great way to start the process of exploring the past. You can write this out, or, if you prefer a more linear way of thinking, take a piece of regular or banner paper and draw a straight line from one end to the other. Start at the left side with a hatch mark that represents your entry into grade school, and then make subsequent marks for high school, college, postgraduation, and adulthood. Be as creative as you want in elaborating on the details of each time period, including:

- Your friends at each stage: what they brought into your life, and what you gave them in return
- Conflicts with significant females, including family
- An assessment of your self-esteem
- Your relationship style at key points: childhood, adolescence, young adult, and so on

After you've filled in significant events, score each one using a scale of 1 to 5, with 5 representing the most aggressive and 1 equaling the least. Take as long as needed to complete the timeline, and feel free to use words and images to illustrate the answers to each point listed. If you're artistic or poetic, you can embellish further! Try to complete a segment representing a specific time period and then progress to the next one in chronological order. Once you're finished, roll up the timeline and put it away for a week or so.

When you feel ready and have a block of time to spend undisturbed, go back and review the timeline. You might even invite someone else to look at it with you to see if there are certain relationship trends and themes in your past—most likely there will be. If you reach the conclusion that you've put yourself in the victim role in relationships again and again, or if you see a pattern where friends come in and out of your life frequently, or numerous conflicts, you have information that can lead to a plan for change. At a minimum, this exercise will help you understand yourself better and identify relationship pros and cons you need to sort out.

Speaking Truth

Linda H. is an accomplished and energetic mother who also volunteers as an advocate for teen girls. One day, while attending a lecture on relational aggression, she listened to stories of how girls hurt each other and found tears streaming down her own face. In amazement, she wondered why on earth she was so upset to hear about bullying among teens, which led to further self-reflection. Linda then realized there was an incident from her youth that she had never fully processed. Putting pen to paper, she wrote about a time in high school when she was not only excluded from a friend's sleepover party, but the girls who did attend trashed her house with rotten vegetables during the night. In sharing this story with others, she was surprised to discover how many details remained clear in her mind so many years later.

Although Linda's story was from the distant past, it still had the power to move her deeply. Imagine how much power recent events have to wound a woman who doesn't understand why she has been targeted.

The Fear Factor

In sifting through your RA history, it's helpful to keep in mind the interaction style of yourself as well as others. Any woman involved in RA shares an underlying fear and lack of self-esteem that leads her to respond as bully, victim, or in-betweener. See if you can identify and understand how specific experiences from the past still shadow your present-day encounters. Subtle feelings, such as a sense of insecurity in certain places, being intimidated by certain situations, or having particular women set your nerves on edge, should make you dig deeper to see if your history is haunting you. Are you reliving math class anxieties or worrying about the moment when everyone strips after a workout and jumps in the shower? Are you having flashbacks of the head cheerleader who bullied you throughout football season, or do long-ago threats of physical violence make you respond negatively to certain women?

Name It

Regardless of whether a woman acts aggressively or passively, there is usually a key behavior inside that leads her to feel wounded. You've probably discovered your emotional Achilles' heel: betrayal, exclusion, humiliation, harassment, or something else—the list is long, but reviewing it can help you identify feelings that trigger present-day hurts.

When thinking intensely about and even reliving events that traumatized you, it's not unusual to feel a variety of emotions. Sometimes a sense of anger ranges from mild upset to raging fury. This may be the same unrecognized emotion that drives your everyday aggression or passivity. For other women, feelings of regret, grief, and sadness can be devastating. Expressing these emotions in ways that are not hurtful to yourself or others can be accomplished by:

- Talking to a friend or a therapist
- Redirecting them into another activity such as exercise
- Using relaxation techniques
- Taking positive action to change the situation or yourself

Whatever you choose, I encourage you to have a "crisis plan" handy should the feelings you go through overwhelm or overpower you. Call a "safe" person whom you feel comfortable turning to for help, or look in the phone book for a crisis hot line.

Share It

Writing about trauma is another powerful tool for expressing and releasing emotions that have collected inside but have never been acknowledged. In several studies, a surprisingly small amount of writing about past stressors improved both physical and psychological health in a number of ways. There are a several options for writing feelings that may be troubling you:

1. Select a specific painful incident, and describe it in detail. Then go back and rewrite how you would handle the situation today.

2. Imagine a Queen Bee who has been particularly troublesome for you. If she is now an adult, write about her as a child. If she was a child when she hurt you, describe her as an adult. Go on to ponder how she might be freed of her RA-style of interacting.

3. Write a letter to yourself about a particularly difficult experience you had with RA. Offer several reasons why you think the event was so hurtful and convince yourself of the importance of letting go of the harm that was done to you.

4. Think of a Queen Bee who has troubled you. Write a story about her "fight for the hive" with another equally powerful Queen Bee.

5. Make a list of words that describe relationship skills you wish you had. Go on to write a story about a recent or past interaction that was difficult, and use those words to describe yourself.

Writing to your tormentor, even as a self-contained exercise, is another way to work on resolving the negative residual of RA. The following letter was very cathartic for the writer, even though she never put it in the mail.

Dear Lynne:

I imagine at this very time in your new job you are busy hurting women in much the same way as you hurt me. Of course, you don't see it as hurting, you see it as "guiding," even being a leader, but make no mistake about it, you are one of the most destructive women I've encountered in twenty years of professional life.

When you came to the university, I was one of your biggest supporters. I remember being hopeful that you would be a strong leader, and that our entire department would make tremendous progress under your guidance. When I saw the "old timers" begin to leave one by one, I should have suspected that you had an agenda of your own. Of course, in every university certain people leave when new administration comes, but under your rule, our department was bulldozed. That's when you set your sights on me.

How could you know that I've always prided myself on being a team player, the person who helps others and goes out of her way to mentor and advocate for junior faculty and students? Somehow you figured this out and used it against me. I'll never forget the day when you made an appointment to see me—in *my* office of all places! I actually thought you might be stopping by to tell me you appreciated my efforts or to chat about the future of our department. It probably wasn't a coincidence that you came to see me shortly after my mother died, when my spirits were low, but what a shocker it was when you began to tear me apart bit by bit, as if I was a sheet of paper you were determined to reduce to the tiniest pieces possible.

Well, you did. By the time our hour was done, I didn't recognize myself in the person you described. How could I be as conniving and disloyal as you portrayed me? You went on your merry way after destroying me, but I lost all confidence in myself at that point.

Ironically, just a few weeks after our talk, the chair of another department contacted me and asked if there was any chance I'd come to work for him. Clearly, he didn't see me in the same light that you did. After interviewing with him and seeing how valuable he considered me to be, the choice to work with him wasn't hard. It was sad to leave a department I had loved with not even an official good-bye.

All these years later, I understand that your underlying problem was insecurity. You cannot stand to be surrounded by strong women, and so you systematically get rid of anyone you think fits that description. We've all done well since leaving you. And you? Well, you were ousted, too, by a new dean who somehow figured out your style and sent you packing. Unlike me, you were demoted rather than promoted. The unfortunate thing is not that you lost your status, but that you got another administrative position in a smaller university, where you have the ability to do to other women the very same things you did to us.

Sincerely,

Cassandra

Cheryl—I've had this typed and printed out for some time now, but have never sent it to Lynne. Maybe someday I will.

Art for the Heart

Some women write songs, paint pictures, sculpt, or create some other form of art to capture, explore, and express their feelings. Whether you choose one of these formats or speak your story in another way, the important behavior is for you to recognize the incident for what it was (RA) and strip the memory of its power to hurt you. Even speaking about past events to a few select friends and having your feelings validated can be surprisingly helpful. Incidents that have wounded you may seem trivial on the surface, but if they caused hurt, they need attention and resolution.

Rituals or symbolism are other ways to release painful memories and let go of residual anger and resentment. You can shred the Relationship Timeline you developed and start a new one beginning with today. Give yourself a gift to celebrate the transition out of RA, or make a pilgrimage to free yourself of specific events or people. You may go back to the high school where you were tormented as a freshman and make your peace with the experience. Writing out short- and long-term goals that will lead to RA-free relationships can give you a concrete action plan focused on the future rather than the past.

The ancient Chinese joss paper ceremony is a way to visibly rid yourself of the past. Joss paper is a special paper used to clear away specific problems and bring new energy into a person's life; you can write down your hurts on the beautiful paper, then burn it and scatter the ashes.

When and How to Confront

The letter written by Cassandra to Lynne brings up a good question: when should you confront others about the past? In her book *I Thought We'd Never Speak Again*, the noted author Laura Davis talks about the process of making peace with relationships that were traumatic. She suggests that before you confront someone, you should take a personal inventory of your own emotions, resentments, and regrets. Balance the benefits and costs of continuing to keep the conflict unresolved. While it may seem unlikely that RA has benefited you in any way, perhaps in your role as victim you have received sympathy or admiration from others, or the unresolved anger that drives your Queen Bee aggression may have fueled your rise up the corporate ladder. It's easier to see the cons of RA as you examine the negative outcomes of your current relationships, frustrations over missed opportunities, loneliness, and the continual fear and anxiety you are likely to battle.

Davis suggests that you ask yourself how far into the future you believe this unresolved relationship issue will continue to affect you. If your aggression or passivity is an escalating problem or is spilling over to taint other areas of your life such as leisure time or family, there is a greater impetus to change.

Once you've decided to take action, try to obtain some sort of validation of the trauma. Check your diary, if you keep one, or reconstruct the events of the situation with the help of others. If there were witnesses, you might ask them if their perceptions were the same as yours. These questions can help you decide whether to proceed to seek out and connect with the person or persons who harmed you in the past.

If you do decide to talk with that person (whether to confront her as a victim or apologize as an aggressor), plan the event carefully. Think ahead on what you hope to accomplish by meeting with the other woman, and rehearse how you will approach the situation. Try to pick a neutral place where neither of you are likely to become hostile and aggressive. Go over the principles of effective communication ahead of time (see appendix A), and remember to listen as well as talk. Avoid blame, and if you're too emotional to meet with the person without exploding, postpone the confrontation.

A letter can sometimes be a helpful way to arrange for a meeting with someone from your past, as can e-mails, because they allow you to communicate without becoming visibly distraught. In either case, wording is critical. If you're going to e-mail, review tips on "netiquette" to avoid online aggression, which is often accidental but frequently instigates online RA, a situation I call cyberslamming (see appendix C).

The following is a summary of dos and don'ts to keep in when you choose to meet with a woman who hurt you in the past. The chances of reaching resolution and closure are greater if you take the time to prepare and rehearse.

Do:

- Allow adequate time for a conversation
- Find a place to meet that is comfortable for both of you

- Treat her with respect
- Set time limits on the meeting when you arrange it
- Practice ahead of time with a friend or your mirror
- Make sure you are physically and emotionally healthy when you schedule the meeting
- Thank her for meeting with you

Don't:
- Interrupt
- Change subjects abruptly
- Use sarcasm
- Use gestures that might be misinterpreted as aggressive or dismissive
- Accuse

Bit by Bit

Don't be surprised if you confront an aggressor and don't receive an apology or forgiveness. In the same way, if you are meeting with a woman you victimized, it shouldn't be surprising to have your words received with bitterness or even anger. In either case, remember that this arranged conversation with a former aggressor or victim is an opportunity for you both to be freed of painful memories, not an occasion for further RA.

Resolution

After recognizing and expressing feelings you've experienced because of an RA situation, take the opportunity to try to come to some kind of resolution. Resolution exists on a continuum and may involve simply acknowledging past traumas or a profound sense of peace and closure. In either situation, it's important for both of you to feel satisfied with the outcome, even if it isn't the ideal one you hoped for. A victim has triumphed if she can confront an aggressor and speak her truth. For an aggressor to admit her behavior was hurtful is also an accomplishment. If you can't get to the point of seeing some gain from the meeting, a professional therapist might enable you to make more progress.

In the following poem, one woman achieves some closure by rationalizing the behavior of another. This enables the author to achieve a sense of peace about their relationship (or lack thereof), which, although not ideal, is still progress.

Her Hatred

BY KATHRYN KIRKPATRICK

Her lip curled. I could see
that she hated me.
It was odd
how the hatred went on
for days and days and years and years.
I began to feel I could
count on it. It was a steady
reliable hatred. Not like
baled hay
which can rot.
Or a hollyhock
which a woodchuck
can whittle to twig.
Her hatred was solid and determined
like petrified wood.
And though it needed no tending,
she tended it.
For instance,
she never spoke to me,
for fear, perhaps, I would damage the hatred
soil its purity, its utter rightness.
But certainly she spoke of me
to others, to shine up the hatred,
to make it glow.
So that finally I felt
her hatred was her gift
and when she offered it up,
I thanked her, silently,
for the strange vigil she kept with it
knowing at last she had nothing else,
nothing else to give.

CHAPTER 14

The Power of Forgiveness

Forgiveness is the key to action and freedom.
—Hannah Arendt

Sometimes the best resolution for RA can be to forgive the perpetrator of long-ago hurts. While it's easy to give lip service to the concept of forgiveness, it's much harder to actually engage in it. The suggestions in the previous chapter may seem woefully inadequate to compensate for a grievous transgression that altered your life for the worse, or they may not work for you. There may be hurts in the past that simply can't be resolved, no matter how hard you try. The idea of forgiveness can be the least palatable alternative yet.

Forgiveness is always an alternative, but all too often we hesitate to let go, choosing instead to hang on to hurts because to set them free feels like defeat or passivity. In my work with young women, I often hear stories about planned retaliations (that is, aggression of some kind) against a girl who has been hurtful. The most often voiced rationale for inflicting emotional harm on the aggressor is: she deserves it.

"Why should I forgive her?" Jo asked me recently, after describing a classmate's mean behavior. "I didn't do anything wrong! This is all her fault." Jo's rage continued for several sessions of our program until she came to realize her aggressor was in the midst of a major family crisis. In the absence of a full-fledged resolution, Jo decided forgiveness was the best option—even if her aggressor never knew it had been given.

Another time, Lee, a high school senior, spoke at length about a girl who harassed her throughout their freshman year for no discernable reason. Face set in a scowl, Lee assured me she would *never* forget—or forgive—her bully's cruelty. When I asked what it was costing her to hang on to her hurt and anger, Lee's face crumpled. "A lot," she admitted.

Of course, at any age it's logical to assert that wrongdoers deserve punishment. When we are on the receiving end of cruel behavior, it's only natural to want to strike back in some way. Many a victim who sits passively seething after an encounter with a Queen Bee and/or Middle Bee dreams of revenge, and some act on those fantasies. A good number of Queen Bees are actually caught up in their own endless replay of a damaging dynamic from the distant past, still unable to let go of fear and hurt. When the RA wounds are deep and transgressions grievous, it's sometimes easier to hold on to the painful feelings associated with bullying than to work free of them.

Unforgivable Women

Everyone meets a variety of unpleasant people in the course of a lifetime. Sometimes that person is a woman so challenging you may wonder if even her mother loved her. If she is an aggressor or an in-betweener who helped to hurt you, the last thing you may want to do is forgive her for the sorrow she caused and possibly never acknowledged. As with Lee, rage and resentment are fuels that will keep the fire of hostility burning brightly, whether you are a victim, a bully, or a bystander.

Holding on to the negative feelings can seem like the best choice—even the *right* choice. The emotion that results from carrying that wound can be energizing, providing a cause to rally around, a reason to receive sympathy from others, and even a way to live your life. In the end, however, withholding forgiveness from a woman who has wronged you is a no-win game.

One problem with refusing to forgive is that your transgressor may not even be aware of the slight she inflicted on you. Misunderstandings and assumptions are leading causes of relational conflict. One woman, who never went beyond high school, assumes her female neighbor with a graduate degree in engineering deliberately snubs her because of the difference in their educational status. Another woman judges a coworker's behavior as arrogant based on her skin color. The president of your women's organization manipulates you into doing her job. In each of these cases, it's easy to harbor resentment that can go on indefinitely, based on superficial impressions.

What if the assumptions are wrong, though? What if that highly educated woman is painfully shy? What if the woman of a different ethnicity is afraid she won't be accepted by others and compensates by excluding them first? What if your president thinks you enjoy doing parts of her job because someday you hope to be in a leadership position?

In each situation, underlying assumptions and failure to communicate openly and honestly set the stage for RA and hurt feelings that can last for decades. They also can prevent you from enjoying new relationships because you are still harboring resentments over old painful ones. Failing to forgive because of a false assumption you formed years ago and refuse to let go of can poison your present-day life, saturating your personality with a negativism and bitterness that will lead others to exclude you.

Casting off skewed perceptions and old hurts can be one of the most empowering activities you do for yourself and others. The author of the following story learned just how much her failure to forgive cost her—luckily before it was too late.

Reunion

Wyndham Bearden

It's my ten-year college reunion and I'm standing under a teal and white tent pitched in a muddy field in upstate New York. The music is blaring and really bad beer is flowing over the sides of wobbling plastic cups. At every turn, I see another face from long ago, some sorely missed, others dismissed. It's overwhelming.

And then I see the back of her head at the other end of the tent. My heart catches and a thudding sound reverberates inside me. I've thought about her repeatedly in the months leading up to tonight, wondered if she'd be here, wondered if she'd acknowledge me if we did meet. I even dreamt about it.

It's been eight years since we last spoke. She was my first college friend, and a good one at that. After graduation, we roomed together in New York, fumbling through first jobs and post-college dating. I couldn't have survived that year without her—oh, how she could make me laugh!

But then she started dating John, our neighbor, a guy whose only asset was his proximity. I liked him even less with her. She was uncharacteristically reserved around him.

A few months into the relationship, she confessed that he was verbally abusive, making her, an attractive, intelligent woman, feel insignificant. It made me mad. I wanted to hurt him, to make him feel small and ugly.

Thankfully, I had just enough sense to realize that wasn't my place. This was her life. I needed to help her—a mission I wrongfully interpreted as convincing her to do what I thought was best: break up with the bastard.

I patiently listened to her tales of their unhealthy union. I tamed my urges to yell, "Dump him!" and talked about taking care of herself, even if that meant being alone. But months turned into a year and then two. By this time, I had moved to Boston, she to San Diego. We talked on the phone often, always about how much he hurt her, even with three thousand miles between them.

But they stayed together. After each of our conversations, I would hang up the phone overflowing with rage and spend the rest of the night fuming. Why couldn't she end it? She didn't even like him, physically or otherwise.

It was exhausting. I began focusing on how tormented I was and quickly lost touch with what should have been my guiding principle: this wasn't about me. But my thought process was muddled, distorted by emotion.

Then one night, she said it. "He makes me feel like a geisha girl." And that was it. Choking on anger, I made a snap judgment, the logic of which is lost on me now, though it was crystal clear then. I would cut off contact with her. I had become an enabler, in spite of myself. Losing me would make her end her relationship with John.

We talked for another hour that night. I comforted her as best I could. As we ended the conversation, I pledged to call her soon, really soon. I told her to take care of herself and hung up.

I never called and stopped returning her calls. I told myself this was the best thing for her—not that I had the guts to tell her that. As far as she knew, I had blown off our six-year friendship for no apparent reason.

I didn't know that night how much my decision would haunt me in the years to come. After all, what would I have done five years ago if my friends had vanished as I shrunk my body down to a 104-pound reed? They had had countless conversations with me about my eating disorder. I could feel the frustration—and love—in their voices as they expressed concern for my welfare. What if they had done as I had? What if they had abandoned me?

As I look around at those very friends, standing in this same muddy field under a teal and white tent, I hold back tears of gratitude and sorrow, love and regret. I go get myself a cup of beer at the other end of the tent, where she's immersed in conversation. My heart's beating hard, but I can't let myself wimp out, not again. I finally approach.

"Hi, it's great to see you," I say.

We hug, and all I can think is: Hi, old friend. I'm so sorry. I've missed you so incredibly much.

Forgiveness is a choice that costs nothing unless you choose to make it expensive. Consider whether there are women in your life who could benefit from the release of a long-ago hurt, and help to make it happen. Whether you offer or accept forgiveness, the gift of new chances is one of the most precious a person can receive.

Compassion

Compassion, a close companion to forgiveness, has many different definitions. Most refer to the notion of understanding what it might be like to be another person. We feel compassion for mothers who are poor, because we can well imagine how difficult it would be to raise children on a low income. Our hearts reach out to women who are victims of violence, because their hurts could easily be ours.

How far does your compassion-ability stretch? Can you extend the same feelings of empathy and caring to women who are not so different from you—women you meet at home, work, and play who might use RA in their interactions with you? How about the aggressive Queen Bee boss who makes your life miserable every day?

Returning to the example of a highly educated female engineer who is also painfully shy, consider what her life might have been like. Her degree is one that probably positioned her as the sole female in her workplace for many years. Try to envision how difficult it must have been for her to have to prove herself again and again. Try to feel how challenging it would be to speak up in a work environment that may well be discriminatory or hostile. In many ways, this woman is a hero, but to others she may seem cold, haughty, and standoffish. Meeting her for the first time, another woman might be inclined to cut her off or buzz about her in the coffee room.

Now imagine that you are that woman, and since childhood, you have found it difficult to express yourself to others. At work, you are forced to fight for every accomplishment and confronted at every opportunity with the demand to be twice as good as the men who surround you. You have learned not to depend on other women because there simply are none at your job. Years later, when more women enter the field of engineering, you lack the skills it takes to build networks with female colleagues. You may still be operating within the male paradigm of leadership, and yes, you may even be aggressive and curt to other women at times. It's not that you intend to hurt others, it's just the way you have learned to survive in a hostile environment.

Challenging yourself to feel compassion for this woman and her counterparts in religious and volunteer organizations, or at the gym, the school, or the supermarket, can be a helpful reframing activity. It probably won't make you want to have lunch with them or step forward to be on committees they chair, but imagining the despair that is driving their behavior may make you more comfortable in situations in which you are forced to be together. It might even motivate you to try to help them learn needed relationship skills.

Recognizing that the woman who aggresses against you acts from a particular frame of reference shows that her hostility, undermining, or manipulation is not about you—it's about her and the life circumstances with which she has had to deal. Perhaps she grew up in a family with many sisters, where aggression and competition were the norm, or perhaps she had no sisters and never learned how to negotiate with other women. Maybe she is the oldest child who learned early on that her parents expected her to achieve at the expense of others, or she may have been the quiet younger sibling who found it pointless to try to defend herself. The facts of her past may place a woman's present-day aggression into a context that helps you understand and even feel compassion for her.

The following story illustrates how compassion can be a viable option for overcoming the harmful intent of RA.

Waving at Miss Velma

LANITA BRADLEY BOYD

When my father and mother went into the general store down the road from their house for a routine purchase of some staple items, the scene was familiar—middle-aged Velma, daughter of the storeowner, sitting with her mother to pick up store gossip. This day, however, Velma rose from her seat, verbally attacking Mother, yelling, "Who do you think you are, making my little Bobby Joe stand in the corner today? Some teacher you are! Picking on my poor little boy!"

Mother had had a hard day with her fourth grade students and at that moment had no memory of what had precipitated the punishment. She stood there as Velma progressed to obscenities that sent mothers with young ones scurrying from the store.

When Mother and Daddy got home—both having taken the abuse in silence—she said, "Lawrence, I'm never going to that store again."

"You don't really mean that," he responded. He knew her well. By morning, she had resolved to turn the situation around.

I think I need some cheese, she decided that afternoon on the way home from school.

She went back to the store, where she was helped by Velma's father, John. Mother, only twenty-one years old, decided to address the situation directly. She said, "Mr. John, I don't care for what happened here yesterday."

Mother thought that was the end of it. But when she got home from the store, Daddy came in, shaking his head.

"Here's our cream," he said. "It wasn't picked up."

In their rural 1944 community, Velma's husband was the local dairy driver who picked up farmers' cream and took it to the dairy every morning. He had left theirs at the side of the road to sour.

After that, they had to take it to the dairy themselves, and soon they quit selling cream, for the long trip every day was more trouble than it was worth. Instead, they simply gave it to neighbors.

Beginning that day, Mother started a determined campaign. Every time she saw Velma or her husband, Alfred, she would smile and say hello. If she were in the car, she would give a big wave. Frequently, she would write positive notes about Bobbie Joe, and she showered him with love and concern.

Toward the end of the school year, Alfred flagged Mother down at the edge of his driveway, catching her in mid-wave. Oh, no, she though. What now?

"Miss Mary," he said, the words tumbling out as though if he paused he might lose courage. "Miss Mary, down at the dairy we have this new kind of oleomargarine. It's colored yellow, and it's in sticks." He shoved a package at her. "I thought you might like to try some." And he was gone.

Two weeks later, he flagged her down again. This time he held a cardboard cylinder. Thrusting it at her, he said, "These here are canned biscuits. Ever hear of that? No, I didn't figger you did. Thought you might like to try them."

Mother had made a point that Miss Velma's husband, at least, had responded to. But this woman of courage and zeal did not stop there.

As the years passed, Mother and Daddy had three children of their own. We children knew nothing of the original conflict between Mother and Miss Velma. All we knew was that Mother would remind us to "wave at Miss Velma, children" every time we passed her house, whether or not we could see her.

I never understood what I perceived as my mother's fondness for this bitter, tight-lipped woman. Sometimes, as the oldest child, I'd be the one sent to Miss Velma's door with the message, "Here's some coconut cake Mother thought you'd enjoy," or "Mother thought maybe you could use these extra tomatoes since we have a good crop this year." But most of the time, it was Mother herself who went to the dreaded door, smiling all the way up the front walk.

After I married and lived out of state, I rarely saw Miss Velma, though sheer habit brought a wave every time I occasionally passed her house. Sometimes Mother would mention that Miss Velma had given her a quilt top, or some preserves, or some purchased gift.

One day when I was at Mother's, Miss Velma, stooped and trembly, stopped by for a visit.

"You know, Lanita, your mama is the finest woman that ever lived," she said. "I've never had a friend like her—ever. I never had a sister, either, but if I'd had one, I'd have wanted her to be just like Mary. You're a lucky young woman to have a mother like her."

I agreed but didn't think much of her comments at the time. After she left, Mother decided to tell me the history of their friendship. "I do love her now," Mother said, "but there were many years when I didn't."

Now, as I encounter difficult people in a variety of situations, my natural tendency is to turn away and deal with them as little as possible, but remembering the example of my mother, I remind myself not to give up but instead to "wave at Miss Velma."

Apologies Accepted

Another aspect of forgiveness and compassion is recognizing when you have wronged another—deliberately or not. As part of changing your relational style, you may need to offer as well as receive apologies for the past, and continue to be on the lookout for times when you accidentally offend. Consider the experiences of this author.

Fourth Grade Bully
LANITA BRADLEY BOYD

I was excited about transferring to fourth grade and looked forward to working with Lucy, having heard so much about what a fantastic teacher she was. We were about the same age, and each of us had a son, a daughter, and a loving husband. I thought we'd really hit it off.

My relationship dream was quickly shattered, because Lucy soon made it clear she did not intend to share anything with me—ideas, equipment, space—nothing. I tried to be the first to offer what I'd read or done, hoping that if I exchanged ideas so would she, but it didn't work.

I noticed that she did not come to the teachers' dining room but stayed in the lounge at lunchtime. To give us some time together, I started bringing my lunch and joining her two days a week. Soon she started staying in her classroom for the duration of every lunch period.

The more I got to know her, the more astonished I was at the high regard in which students and parents held her. Her comments and questions in faculty meetings often brought sidelong glances and even snickers from the other teachers. Unfortunately, I, too, was guilty of being amused by her responses.

"I need to talk to you in the teachers' lounge," Lucy said tightly one afternoon.

Meekly, I followed. Closing the door, she turned to me, eyes blazing. "I cannot believe the way you treated me in the faculty meeting yesterday!" she began. "When I asked about the transparencies with that machine, you looked around and rolled your eyes! That was so hateful!

"I just can't take it any more! You thrust yourself into this grade against my wishes and then are so pushy and arrogant about all your ideas. Always telling me something you've read or something you're doing—and wanting to copy my ideas as well. And you're always yelling at me!

"I can tell you, I've had it! You constantly humiliate me in front of the students. Even when we weren't teaching the same grade, you would rarely speak to me in the hall. I'd be leading a class down the hall and we'd meet you and I'd say, 'Hello, Mrs. Boyd!' and you'd just give that little tight-lipped smirk and go on. One day a child even asked, 'Why didn't Mrs. Boyd speak to you?' and I didn't know what to say!"

At this point, I started to say that I usually speak to people the first time I see them for the day and after that just smile as we meet—that it seemed artificial to me to speak jovially at every hall encounter, as she did. I didn't know what she meant by "tight-lipped smirk," but decided I'd better use a mirror to analyze my smile. Fortunately, I sensed that it was not the time for rebuttal. I stood there in silence, trying to look humble and contrite.

After she finished her barrage, I simply apologized. I explained that I bore her no ill will—had, in fact, looked forward to teaching with her. Trying to word it differently each time, I apologized again and again—for intruding, for being unfriendly, for being overbearing, for existing.

When we finally left, both exhausted, I had no idea what would come of our situation. As it turned out, that was only one of several similar confrontations. With each one, I learned more about the multitude of actions that offended her and how to get along without giving in to her bullying techniques. I learned to quietly make one point in each conversation and let it go at that. "I only shared ideas in hopes that you would share ideas with me—not that I thought mine were better than yours."

I also learned that sometimes she was right. "I don't mean to be yelling at you. I forget to leave my classroom voice behind."

We eventually taught fourth grade together for ten years, with a better relationship each year. I understood why so many teachers had left that position, but I refused to be driven away by Lucy, the oldest fourth grade bully I'd ever known.

It takes both courage and integrity to admit you've wronged another. This past year I designed a schoolwide "forgiveness" activity for girls in grades six to eight. Shortly after these young women were offered the opportunity to write a letter asking for or offering forgiveness to another girl, thirteen-year-old Megan flagged me down at an assembly.

"Dr. Dellasega, I wrote that letter," she told me with the kind of exuberance only adolescent girls possess. "And I actually gave it to the person I wrote about." (That part was optional.) Her smile showed every one of the braces on her teeth as she concluded, "I feel so much better!" At a young age, Megan learned a lesson that can be valuable for many, and she probably found it easier to discuss forgiveness than many adults would.

The pain of RA can continue to taint your life as long as you live, if you let it. In order to open new doors of opportunity for yourself, admit to and let go of past or present aggression, both the episodes you know of and those that you may be unaware of. (By the way, if there's anyone I may owe an apology to at this point, please consider it given—and contact me if we need to discuss it further!) Once this is done, you will feel free to move on and create new relationship styles that are healthier and happier for both you and the women around you.

CHAPTER 15

The Won't Bee

She's just like that woman in the song—a killer queen.
—A MAN TALKING ABOUT A QUEEN BEE

I t's one thing to talk about situations involving RA in which you have some measure of control: the volunteer group you can restructure or quit, the job you have the ability to walk away from, or the woman you can forgive and then forget. What happens when you are stuck—literally unable to remove yourself either mentally or physically from a situation in which you find your worst bullying tendencies coming out or your strongest victim behaviors accented?

What do you do when forgiveness is not a realistic or viable option? Even the best laid action plan and most polished behavior-change program simply can't budge the Won't Bees of this world. Won't Bees, as you have probably guessed, are women who make life miserable for everyone around them—no matter what.

How do you deal with a difficult relationship when you've done everything possible to make it better without success? While some of the experts I spoke with suggested that there is never a situation that can't be reversed, in reality there are single mothers, primary-breadwinner mothers, immobile women, and others who would risk serious financial or emotional crises if they left situations solely to avoid other women. These are situations in which ongoing contact makes forgiveness impossible. What can you do when you're forced into continued contact with unpleasant women who make it their mission to keep aggression in your life?

Develop Alternatives

Rose, an attractive, middle-aged human resources manager I spoke with, discussed female aggression on and off the job.

It was not unusual to have female employees come to me in tears, just really broken, because other women made it their business to circulate rumors, such as they were having affairs with their bosses. I can think of several situations where there were other women who were making it their business to just spread these very, very damaging rumors, and I guess it has just been my position over the years, wherever I am, to have a very, very low threshold for rumors and gossip because they are so damaging.

I try to get women to approach the individuals who are gossiping and say to them, "I am really disturbed by the things that you are saying because there is no truth in them." My experience has been that nonprofessionals tend to be very reluctant to do this. But short of that, I tell them to demonstrate to their aggressors, almost go overboard, to avoid anything that might be viewed as a compromising situation. Anytime you are sitting there with your boss, make sure the doors are open. You know, if they don't like the fact that maybe at lunchtime the two of you go on a walk, ask them to go along, or maybe for a period of time just don't do that anymore. Those are some of the things that I would suggest for them to do. When the boss is aware, I have a little more flexibility and can work on team-building activities.

I also make a point to say, "You have got to hold your head up high." I feel very strongly about that, and tell them that the minute your body language shows that you are just crushed, then you start coming across as though what they are saying about you is true. You have got to project yourself very confidently, you hold your head up, you do your work, you are very conscientious about your job, you are doing your job every day and really impress that upon them in those situations.

Other strategies suggested by contributors for getting around women who block you, regardless of whether the behavior occurs in a gym or the boardroom, include:

- Ignore them.
- Persist despite them.
- Find alternate routes to success.
- Maintain a positive attitude.
- Avoid giving them any ammunition to use against you.
- Connect with other women who are also feeling "blocked."

Survive, Thrive, and Feel Alive

In the midst of an onslaught of behavior that threatens in one way or another, any woman can respond with either aggressive or passive behavior. For women stuck in a relationally aggressive dynamic, it's important to remember that the impressions of others do not ultimately determine who you are and what you will make of your life.

Debra Mandel, Ph.D., a clinical psychologist and the author of *Healing the Sensitive Heart*, works with many women in her private practice. She talks about the dynamic of RA, suggesting:

I think it often shows up more in the workplace, where competition is an issue. In intimate relationships, usually women have done preliminary work with selecting friends. Healthier women who have dealt with their issues are more likely to have healthier relationships with friends.

But women who feel victimized will often pick relationships with other people who re-create the same relationships. If your role was to be passive and meek to ward off an abusive parent, you will often get into relationships with women where someone bullies you. The woman who is passive may sabotage the relationship by avoiding calls, being secretive, and bad mouthing her friend without ever directly expressing her feelings.

But women often treat themselves the same way they allow another person to treat them—as though they don't have value. They are their own worst enemy. Learning how to set boundaries *lovingly* is the key. When victims recognize that they've been victimized, they'll often overcompensate and show up like a bull in a china shop. The bully is one step ahead, because she's got entitlement and may feel she can hurt others who have hurt her. She has to recognize that the most empowerment she'll feel is through setting boundaries lovingly.

Set a boundary by recognizing what your own needs and feelings are; verbalize in "I" statements, leaving off blame and shame of other people; say things like: "Joanne, when you raise your voice to me, I feel angry, I feel hurt. When you do that I'm going to choose to not listen. I would like to have a conversation at another time."

Fully claim responsibility for your own feelings but realize you can't control others. What we perceive as abusive is only abuse because we don't have the strength to fend it off. For example, at work, the ultimate choice is to leave the job, but let's say a woman can't leave. Internally set your own boundaries, and know what your ultimate limits are. For example, if anyone is throwing or hitting, you may be out of there. What is the bottom line for you? Is this person triggering some old wounds? Is this person like your mom or a teacher who shamed you? If that's true, you'll be having the relationship as though you're a wounded child. Sometimes this helps us let things roll off without having to stick.

Let's say your mom called you stupid as a child. In reality you are accomplished, attractive, and intelligent. So that is an old wound, not a truth. But let's say you get with a boss who says you are stupid. You can look at your boss and recognize it's her issue, if you're healed. If you're not healed, it's going to feel abusive.

Recognize that if anything gets so bad, many times as adults we have an exit. Even the single mom who needs to work has resources and outlets for help in this country. Battered women leave, and they're a lot better off even if they're poor, because they made a choice that's life affirming.

If you're in doubt about a situation, do a Relationship Cost Benefit Analysis. Look at what you get and what it costs you. Healthy relationships are ones where we get more, they're not exploitive, and the relationship gives something that makes it worth handling some of the stuff that's not so good. Women blackmail themselves, thinking, I have to keep Susan in my life because she helped me out. But Susan makes you pay a price for that, so it's not a good relationship.

Another strategy to get the best results from a communication around relationship issues is to make sure the other person is in a pretty good place. If she is feeling competitive or in a bad mood, it's unlikely something good will come out of an interaction. Increase the sense of safety for others— don't go up to people and be judgmental and attack them. They won't feel safe, and their response won't be positive— nor will yours.

I've seen so many success stories when women do this work. They have magnificent relationships. For example, a woman I'll call Jennifer had a highly contentious relationship with her sister who was a couple of years older. The older sister was envious and resentful of the accomplishments of Jennifer, who had no idea her sister felt threatened by her.

Once Jennifer cleared out her shame and developed a sense of self-worth, she could approach her older sister. She did this by becoming curious about her sister, saying that despite the fact that they were close in age, it seemed the older sister didn't want to have anything to do with Jennifer, which made her feel victimized. The older sister poured out a litany of things, saying she felt Jennifer was judgmental of her mothering skills and had an attitude that made her feel bad about herself. In surprise, Jennifer responded that she felt she was constantly shielding herself from her older sister's judgments. The two came to respect each other's viewpoints and share time, a dynamic that influenced Jennifer's transformation with other members of her family and some friends.

Staking Your Boundaries

In her article "Stand Up for Yourself!" *Fitness* magazine writer Maryann Hammers draws parallels between self-esteem and boundaries, claiming that when a person is clear on what she expects and will tolerate from others, they treat her more respectfully.

To begin exploring your boundaries, ask yourself the following questions:

- What rules do I have for the behavior of myself and others? (For example, is it okay for others to tease you about your carrot-colored hair, or does that offend you?)

- What feelings let me know when someone has taken advantage of me? (For example, you feel enraged when a friend stands you up in order to meet her abusive ex for a drink.)

- How comfortable am I with physical contact with others? (For example, when you meet an acquaintance, and she closes in for a hug, do you want to run away?)

- What is the absolute bottom line for me in terms of behavior? What are the relationship makers and breakers? (For example, a woman who is disloyal will *always* be erased from your friendship list.)

While Hammers encourages women to begin gradually sharing their newly recognized boundaries with others, she also stresses the importance of flexibility and willingness to negotiate— but only to a point. Standing your ground can be difficult if it's new behavior, but will ultimately help empower you to maintain your expectations of self and others.

Difficult People

In their book *Dealing with People You Can't Stand*, Drs. Rick Brinkman and Rick Kirschner describe a variety of ways for dealing with others who may be aggressive or difficult. First, they suggest slotting the difficult individual into one of ten categories that describes their behavior pattern (for example, the Whiner, the Sniper, or the Grenade). Then they spell out your choices for dealing with such people, which include doing nothing, leaving the situation ("vote with your feet"), or changing your own attitude or behavior. (They don't focus on attempting to change the behavior of the other person.) A particular approach these authors advocate is blending and redirecting, which involves reducing the differences between you and the other person and then trying to change the dynamics of the interactions you have.

Toxic People

A female rabbi who has worked with several synagogue congregations points out that we all realize there are toxic people we just can't be around.

> You can't appoint someone who's toxic to a position of power—that's taking care of ourselves. Really, the basic strategy is to keep this kind of aggression away because it's poisonous. We need to stand up for ourselves to not have abusive people there. One of the things I found out when I dealt with this was that there were a number of significantly unhealthy people who had positions of power, and at the end of the year they had resigned. If you set certain rules, such as you can't yell or say anything that's unkind, these people just drop away. This is one of the things I've talked to my rabbinical colleagues about, and we've all come to the same conclusion: in the presence of health, the unhealthy people fall away. So one strategy for women is to create health: surround the bully with health.
>
> There's also a time when, if you believe that God has something better for you, you look around and say, whoa, this is a toxic environment. You have to have a lot of faith and trust in the umbilical cord of the soul that's not cut from God. One woman I recall, who was so harsh and judging of others, had a boss who was a toxic person. She finally realized that she can find another, possibly better, job. She has changed completely from being a person who was so scared and rigid to being much gentler with everything.

Backlash Aggression

The key to dealing with difficult people is to remember the concept of positive confrontations and to avoid dealing aggressively with aggressive people. Choose the time when you will confront her, rather than reacting to an onslaught of verbal abuse from your tormentor with an explosion of your own. This is what the woman in the following story did.

Bullies in the Form of Adult Women

ELIZABETH HILLIARD

Does bullying occur in adult women? Does it occur within a community setting or a workplace environment? You bet it does. I have experienced it first hand

My experience with bullying in adult women happened eight years ago. I was the clerk/business manager in a rural, country school, and the bully was a woman who had been on the board of trustees with two men for roughly five years and then became the chairperson with a whole new board.

I ultimately would call "Bully's" behavior harassment. Had she been able to get the trustees to agree with her, I would have been fired; because she could not, she did everything to get me to quit. She wanted to get rid of me because I knew more than she did, and she was scared of that.

Her bullying began with a phone call one afternoon, shortly after she had taken over as chairperson. I would receive many phone calls from her in the coming year.

In her phone call, she told me that the paraprofessional in the school had complained about me, yet didn't say what had been said. When I approached the paraprofessional about it, that person had no idea what I was talking about. Bully would use this approach over and over throughout the year. Often times I didn't know who allegedly had complained about me, or what the complaint was. The times that I asked, she would brush me off. With time, I did realize that she was lying to me, but because it was always on the phone when I was at home, I had no one to witness it.

A month after she became the chairperson, upon arriving at the school for the board meeting, which takes place in the clerk's office, I found her at my desk, looking through my files. Had something come up missing in these files, I would be blamed. When I asked her, nicely, to move so I could prepare for the meeting (something she knew I did), she blew up. She told me that it was *not* my desk and acted like I had yelled at her, and there was nothing I could do to defend myself. She did move, however, but I was never allowed to say "my" desk or "'my" chair, even though everyone else at the school could. If I slipped up, I would hear about it.

Her phone calls always came in the mornings, sometimes before I was truly out of bed, and usually the morning after a board meeting. Never was I approached in a manner that we could talk civilly, never could I say anything right. During these calls, she would accuse me of not telling her things, not telling the board, of not liking her. Yet when I would try to share information with the board, either she was unreasonably angry over the memo I sent out, or she would let people interrupt me at the board meetings.

The teachers made purchases of $200 or more, and never did she question any of them; yet every one of my purchases, never for over $50, was questioned.

I took this for over a year, despite not being able to sleep or function normally within the community, and despite people telling me to quit. Finally, I realized that I held more cards than she did, and I stood up to her at a board meeting, with the other trustees present. I was polite and calm, but for every accusation, for everything that she tried to put on *my* shoulders, I gave back to her. That was the last time she ever came at me in an angry, unreasonable manner.

Incorporate Stress Management Strategies

You can modify and use stress management strategies for emergency help when dealing with difficult people. Before a difficult RA situation can affect your well-being, put some of the following interventions in place:

- Walk to work, and imagine with each step that you are growing wiser and stronger, and will soon resolve the RA dilemma in which you find yourself stuck.

- Practice deep breathing, which will help you release pent-up stressful emotions. Imagine exhaling all the negative feelings with each out breath. You'll get so good at it you can use this technique anywhere, if only briefly, for stress relief.

- Rehearse assertive communication at home, imagining the woman who is aggressive toward you sitting in a chair but unable to speak back.

- Use yoga or relaxation exercises to keep your body loose and free of tension. You might deliberately exercise right before an encounter with a woman whom you anticipate you will interact with negatively.

When to Get Outside Help

If the difficult person is part of your work environment, you do have recourse to outside help. My husband Paul, an attorney with labor law experience, offers the following guidelines:

1. Read your employee handbook. Look at the grievance or complaint procedure and how it defines harassment vs. sexual harassment so you know what your complaint actually is.

2. If you can phrase your complaint in terms of asserting a right to be free from some type of discrimination, be it age, sex, handicap, race, or national origin, you are protected by federal law from being retaliated against for making a complaint. If you follow an internal grievance procedure, keep copies of all paperwork and make notes about important conversations with decision makers. If your complaint is in the area of a federally protected right (race, sex, age, gender, national origin) consider filing a complaint with the EEOC (Equal Employment Opportunity Commission) or a companion state agency.

3. If you have reported some type of wrongdoing within a company and feel you have been retaliated against, get a copy of your relevant state and federal "Whistle Blower" laws and see whether you qualify as a whistleblower. (A whistleblower is a person who reports wrongdoing and, as a consequence, receives from management some type of adverse employment action, which could be as major as termination or demotion or as minor as a threat.)

4. In many states, Pennsylvania for example, there is a law that permits you to examine your personnel file. If you are concerned about what could be in that file, particularly

negative performance evaluations, ask to see it once a year or more. If, as part of an internal grievance process, you receive an oral communication that you find offensive or potentially contrary to law, either write a note or memorandum to the speaker or your human resources department confirming what was said.

5. All states provide coverage for work-related injuries, but each state's rules are different. Some are very liberal, others, particularly in the South, are not. Some states cover work-related mental or emotional stress injuries, but typically they are harder to prove. If you think you have sustained a work-related injury, call your state Department of Labor and Industry or its equivalent and ask for specific information as to how and when you must report a work injury, how to file a formal claim for benefits, and whether you must use a company doctor for a set period of time. Some states have very short notice requirements, and failure to follow the rules can result in loss of your claim.

6. If you are discharged, contact your local unemployment office, as that likely will be your first and immediate source of benefits since litigated or adversarial proceedings typically take months. If you see a counselor, this strengthens the case for work-related mental distress. Tell him or her your history and obtain a recommendation and diagnosis. If you are offered a choice between being fired and resigning, make absolutely certain that a voluntary resignation does not disqualify you from unemployment benefits. Typically, voluntary quits are disqualified.

Paul goes on to say:

It's very difficult to bring a defamation action as you might want to if someone is slandering you. In most states, opinions can never be defamatory. Only false assertions of fact can be defamatory. An example of this might be if Joan tells her boss that Marie, another employee, had divulged company secrets to a competitor; that's an assertion of a false fact. If Joan told her boss that Marie is a sloppy worker who doesn't give her best effort to her assignments, this is an opinion and, therefore, almost never defamatory. Circulating a false statement of fact, for example, someone is having an affair with her boss, can be defamatory; circulating an opinion that I think they're having an affair, is not. In that situation, you should report the false and malicious rumor to human resources, because, depending on who generated the rumor, it could constitute sexual harassment, even if it involves two women. Sexual harassment complaints as a rule are not actionable unless they first have been reported to your appropriate manager and your company is given an opportunity to act upon them and remedy them. If you are given a performance evaluation you disagree with and are asked to sign the evaluation, don't sign it if you believe it's untrue, unless you're given the opportunity to explain why you believe it's untrue.

Sometimes the prudent course is to seek outside help to resolve certain RA issues. If legal counsel is needed, find an attorney who is experienced in family law, where harassment cases are more common. Your local bar association should be able to provide names.

The Middle Bee

It takes a group to confront and expose the Middle Bee, but she is part of creating the Queen Bee woman who appears to be difficult and hostile. The Middle Bee keeps everyone else in a state of antagonism by using the strategy of "divide and conquer." But rather than stand back and allow the Middle Bee to wreak her damage, potential victims can:

- Agree that no one will share information with her not directly related to the job
- Use neutral language when speaking with her
- Band together to confront her, and speak to the boss

Getting to Goals

Feeling powerless often keeps a victim or bully trapped in a bad position. The bully may feel that if she is less aggressive, she will be unable to maintain her position in whatever organization or community of which she is a member. For the victim, sensing that she has no options but to be passive can keep her stuck in a place that invites further victimization.

How can you get what you need despite the difficult women you may have to deal with? First, examine your own bottom line and establish the values and goals that are most important to you. If being part of a committee chaired by a bully will provide you with entree into an organization you want to cultivate, staying put may be worth it.

On the other hand, if you as a victim are being exploited and harassed to the point of carrying anger and resentment home every day from work, or if you as a bully are so tense and threatened you bully beyond the office, it's time to ask some tough questions: Are you really better off staying in a situation that not only hurts you and, most likely, those around you?

You might be surprised what happens when you communicate your needs clearly and carefully. Donna, the mother of three teenagers and one of several administrative assistants, was continually harassed at work by Eva, the office manager. Everything Donna did was wrong, from handing out the mail to taking phone messages. She tried everything she could think of to free herself from the victim role—forgiveness, refocusing, using exercise to release frustration. Nothing worked. Donna finally reached her limit and decided that even if it meant being unemployed, she was going to resign. When she told Eva her intent, the manager was shocked to hear that her behavior was offensive. "I grew up with five sisters, and I had to fight for everything I got," she told Donna. This began a series of conversations that ended with Donna staying at the job, and Eva reevaluating what she had thought of as leadership behaviors. A few months after Donna took a risk and spoke honestly with Eva, several of the other administrative assistants thanked her for her bravery. They all noticed—and appreciated—having the Won't Bee Eva transformed into a colleague who realized how valuable they each were.

CHAPTER 16

A New Relational You

Finally, after so many years, at last I'm scoring
victories rather than racking up failures.

—LISA LONDON, A FORMER AFRAID-TO-BEE

Reflecting on the past and ridding yourself of hurt can help you begin to change old patterns of behavior, but in order to complete this process, you need a vision for your new relational style. One healthy way to get yourself into the habit of positive relational skills is to make a conscious effort to feel good about yourself and surround yourself with women who reinforce this perception.

Role Models

Up until now, there's been a lot of discussion and description of negative role models: women we don't want to emulate for one reason or another. What about women who can teach you better ways of interacting with your peers?

One way to explore this is to think back over the previous twelve months and identify women who have been significant positive influences for you. It may help to flip back your calendar and refresh your memory on those who came in and out of your life, what they taught you about yourself, and whether you consider them a positive influence.

When you've come up with the names of several women who left you with a good impression (anyone from a therapist you pay to a media figure you admire), look closely at their behavior and figure out what has stayed with you. Is it their objectivity? Their self-assurance? Make a mental or written list of those traits, and then find women in your current life who exhibit them. The goal is to be with others who will bring out the best in you, and with whom you will feel comfortable and relaxed. These women can also reinforce the positive relationship styles you're striving to integrate.

Success Stories

Another strategy for improving self-esteem is to accomplish something new, perhaps in an area you've never attempted before. Open any exercise magazine and read accounts of women who ran their first races or rode their bikes for fifty-mile treks, and you'll get the idea. There are women who changed careers, women who discovered a new talent, and women who reinvented themselves completely. All tried something they never thought they could do and succeeded. Putting yourself in a new context also will give you a second chance to work on behaviors that have previously been problematic.

Safe and Secure

The underlying goal of improving your self-esteem is to make you impervious to those impulses that lead to aggressive behavior or passive acceptance of it. Feeling confident about yourself goes hand in hand with feeling safe. When you are in a comfortable environment with people you trust, you are much less likely to resort to behaviors that will hurt another or yourself.

Begin to identify these kinds of safe places and situations for yourself. They will be different for everyone, but might involve walking on the beach, driving in the car listening to music, talking to your sister on the telephone, shopping with a good friend, or having lunch with a trusted colleague. Whatever the opportunity might be, focus on it intensely. Think of all the details and ask yourself:

- How does my body feel?
- What thoughts are going through my mind?
- What is my behavior like?

- What does the person I'm with do that makes me feel comfortable and secure?
- How often do I feel this way?

Once you have identified the features of these safe situations, you can recreate them for yourself in other settings. You can also promote an inner sense of safety by consciously using the behaviors, the feelings, and the physical sensations you identified in as many situations as appropriate.

Spirituality and Self-Esteem

Hannah, a spiritual director who works with groups of women, sees bullying and victimization as the end products of low self-esteem. She says her goal is to get women to:

> Not just understand but believe in their hearts that God loves them and created them. Once they make the connection, that immediately diminishes the behavior. My first strategy is to learn not to be abusive to the self and learn what abuse is. I tell them they wouldn't let anyone talk to their children like that, so don't say anything to yourself you wouldn't say to a child.
>
> Another strategy is to get rid of the "should" mentality, which so often leads to aggressive behavior. Things like: "You *should* wear a certain kind of clothes," or "You *should* behave in a certain way." In women, aggression comes out of a sense of wanting to control rather than wanting to be mean, and the "shoulds" are a way of getting validation that their way is *the* right way. I ask them, "Who makes these rules? Does God have rules like that?" If you can get someone to laugh at what they're saying and doing, not in a humiliating way, but to lighten something up, it helps. I ask them, "If you have this many rules for others, how many do you have for yourself?" All of this comes from a sense that "I'm not good enough."
>
> One of the most important things one to one or in a group setting is getting women to look at how they take care of themselves. Once I point out that these judgments of other people are mirrors of the kinds of judgments we put on ourselves, they start to get it.

Positive Self-Talk

We all engage in mental chitchat, using this process to solve problems, store information, and work through emotions. There is even a relationship between the way we talk to ourselves and our health, with those people who speak to themselves in positive terms reporting a higher level of wellness. According to a paper published by Julia Weikle, the executive director of Greenbrier Community Services, Inc., in Ronceverte, West Virginia:

> The development of optimistic thought patterns requires essentially three things: recognizing self-talk for what it is, dealing with negative messages, and harnessing the positive for the greater good of individual persons. In a society where people (especially females) are taught to downplay their good points, developing positive self-talk might be difficult at first. It necessitates a "reality-check." Most of the time, people are a lot "better" (performance/health-wise) than they previously concluded. The development of positive personal speech requires that people take active roles in shaping events in their lives, not to let life just "happen to them."

Affirmations are a good example of positive self-talk that can be used to avoid RA. Based on the premise that thoughts influence actions, the voices that run through your head when you feel threatened by another woman are important to examine. What words do say to yourself, and what thoughts are running through your mind when you find yourself in the midst of an aggressive or passive episode?

Reg Connolly, a certified trainer and master practitioner of Neuro-Linguistic Programming (NLP) and a former registered psychotherapist with the United Kingdom Council suggests that internal messages may become a form of negative self-hypnosis, so ingrained we automatically accept the words without really hearing them. If you habitually receive and believe put-downs or typically respond in anger to other women, you may be unconsciously responding with RA. Fortunately, self-talk can be switched from negative to positive. (For more information on negative self-talk, see appendix B.)

Affirmations are deliberate statements you make to yourself in order to harness the inner power of your thoughts in a beneficial way. To create affirmations, use "I" statements, action verbs (can, am, will, do) and positive actions. At a minimum, say them to yourself on a daily basis. Some examples of affirmations you might use to counteract RA tendencies are:

Victim: I am a valuable friend to others. I can speak up and express my opinions in a positive manner.

Bystander: I will be a source of positive energy. Today I will connect women in a way that helps them and me.

Bully: My inner abilities will help me succeed through positive connections with others.

There are several techniques for incorporating affirmations into your daily life: as a mantra, first thing in the morning when you look in the mirror; as reminder notes around your office or home; or by using a rubber band around your wrist. Any strategy that prompts you to remember to give yourself a quick emotional boost through citing an affirmation will work.

Managing Stress

Developing a plan to control stress can also be beneficial, because this is a factor that can often lead aggressors to explode, victims to feel even more harried and unable to cope, and in-betweeners incapable of responding to anything beyond the immediate crises. RA itself is a cause of stress, and when other external events occur that are traumatic, a woman can become emotionally paralyzed or trapped in a cycle of nonstop aggression. For example, if new situations are stressful for a woman who tends to bully, her hostility and aggression may escalate when she's forced into the unfamiliar, which will in turn make coping even more challenging for her and those with whom she has to interact. A victim who dreads a particular committee meeting may become even more passive and reticent when the time comes to attend one, leaving her fellow committee members challenged to work productively with her. Stress-reduction techniques can help in these situations by defusing the stressful perceptions and responses that increase both bullies' and victims' feelings of threat and vulnerability, which in turn escalate the use of RA-type behaviors.

A wealth of resources for stress management can be found on the Internet and in any library or bookstore. After many years of conducting stress management seminars, I can attest to the effectiveness of developing a personal plan for handling stress in even the most impossible situations. Some of the techniques women have found especially beneficial include:

- Journaling
- Deep breathing
- Exercise
- Communicating
- Time management
- Prayer
- Yoga
- Dance
- Guided imagery
- Listening to music

This is just a sampler of strategies that can be used, but the underlying intent of each is to help you pause in the midst of a frenzied time and regroup. If you look over the list, you'll see that each activity offers the opportunity to gain insight about oneself and the situation at hand, either through reflection, movement, or a combination of both.

Another cognitive strategy is to take a Stress Inventory. While there are prepackaged forms to help you with this, it is also possible to explore stress issues in a more flexible way. In identifying challenges around RA and interactions with other women, ask yourself the following questions:

- Am I always stressed by one individual, or do many women make me feel irritated and uncomfortable?
- Are there settings where my tendency toward victimization or aggression seems to come out, for example, at work, at home, or in community organizations?

- What kinds of things go on immediately before I experience conflict with another woman?

- What physical symptoms do I notice when I feel threatened by another woman?

- What are my thoughts and feelings after an encounter with RA?

These questions can get you thinking about stress, as well as the underlying components of your relational esteem. Writing out your responses can be especially beneficial, because you can review them later on and, over time, evaluate the progress you make in modifying them. Give yourself five or ten minutes to write whatever comes into your mind regarding the questions, and don't worry about grammar or spelling. Just pour out your inner thoughts on paper as fast as you can. Later, come back and complete the exercise again and compare your responses over time. For example, in response to the first question, an aggressor might write about feelings Eileen shared with me.

> I am typically stressed by women, never men. There is a certain kind of woman who gets to me, and that is the woman who somehow draws all the attention to herself. Women who wear a lot of makeup bother me the most. I think it signals a preoccupation with appearance that gets to me. There is a woman at my church who comes in every Sunday dressed to kill and layered with makeup. She makes her rounds, greeting everyone, but in reality, showing off, I think. She's not especially attractive, but she has the look of someone who takes good care of herself—obviously! One time our pastor asked the two of us to work on a project together. I was really nasty to her, made comments at every turn about her performance, and suggested she wasn't very bright. None of that was true, but she was obviously so concerned about her image as we worked on the project that she didn't bother trying to collaborate with me.

This is bully talk that assigns the blame for the bully's own insecurities to another person. If this aggressor went on to work with a therapist or a counselor regarding the very telling narrative she just wrote, she might come to some important realizations.

Clearly, she has an immediate and intense stress response to a particular kind of woman that then triggers her worst Queen Bee responses. Once she explores why she is triggered by women she perceives as attention-seeking, something as simple as a few deep cleansing breaths when she feels herself begin to respond physically can be a powerful stress defuser. Alone or with the help of a professional, working on systematically training herself to avoid such negative responses from turning on can also help her get a handle on aggression or passivity.

Walk the Talk

As with any behavioral change, using every opportunity possible will help you refine and internalize healthier relationship styles. Start with the familiar, for example, a woman with whom you have traditionally had an aggressive or passive relationship. Changing the way you interact with her will help both of you explore alternative ways of relating. Perhaps there's a colleague with whom you always gossip about a particular coworker you both dislike, or maybe you've been the victim of a neighbor's manipulating behavior for years. Whatever the dynamic, anticipate how you can act differently—even in a small way— the next time you see this woman. Perhaps you will choose *not* to see her, but then both of you lose the opportunity to share a healthier interaction style.

Walk through the probable scenarios in detail. Your colleague is headed for your desk with her coffee cup. "Let's take a break," she suggests, and you know this is an invitation to update your mutual animosity for the absent coworker. What will you do, now that you realize the trash talk that once seemed so harmless could cause deeply hurt feelings if it reached the ears of your coworker? The choices are endless and limited only by your resourcefulness. The following are a few suggestions that women have come up with that might be used in this situation:

- Change the topic.
- Interject something positive.
- Change the habit (for example, suggest going for a walk instead of sitting with coffee).

- Bring up the subject of relational aggression.

- Develop compassion for the target of your gossip.

- Try to get to know the absent coworker and understand her better.

- Invite a third person with you on the break—someone who doesn't know the coworker and won't participate in gossip.

It's surprising how easy it is to begin with one simple change, which will then gather momentum. Another frequent piece of advice from women seeking to end RA was to have a "zero tolerance" for gossip. While this might seem like an impossible goal, once you sensitize yourself against making hurtful comments and eliminate them from your life, your willingness to accept such talk from others will diminish. You'll be surprised at how good it feels, and what a different perspective it brings to your relationships.

Find the Like-Minded

A middle-aged religious leader of women's groups believes that once we have raised awareness of our aggressive or passive behaviors, the next thing to do is surround ourselves with a group of supportive people who will not interact in ways that were previously damaging. She recalls: "I had a friend with whom I used to go to lunch regularly. We would each tell the awful things going on in our lives during these outings. Three years ago I went out to lunch with her, after a period of not seeing her, and I realized I was no longer interested in talking about everything that was awful in my life."

The same woman goes on to advise that, although gossip can be delicious and can even bond groups of people together, we need to raise our sensitivity to the kind of terrible talk that puts another down, and plan ahead for what to do when the chatter turns catty. She adds the following options to those already listed:

- Remove yourself from the situation.

- Ask for clarification on why the instigator of the gossip is sharing such information.

- Explore the root cause of the other woman's need to be judgmental.

Positive Confrontations

The danger of heightened awareness is that it can lead to overkill. Aggressive behavior can be interpreted as assertive behavior for the victim who has decided to change her passive ways. For a woman who has been an Afraid-to-Bee, the encouragement to begin using strategies that will help express her emotion has the potential to create a backlash bully. Assertive people never seek to have their own needs met at the expense of others, but rather they create a win-win situation that allows both parties to feel recognized. In the same way, Queen Bees who have bullied others into submission need to learn assertiveness skills in order to confront others in ways that lead to the positive resolutions of problems.

Coach Susan Race, founder of Personal Growth Systems located in Wayne, Pennsylvania, and author of *Succeeding in the Workplace: Critical Skills for a Rewarding Career and Life You Love*, often deals with women who need to learn to approach and resolve conflict. She says this about positive confrontations:

> When we come from a place of fear and lack, we lash out at others because we are jealous, envious, and hurting. When we are the recipient of such aggressive behaviors, a positive response is to first ask ourselves what we think is happening, and what makes us willing to assume the guilt and responsibility.
>
> For example, I was working with some corporate employees, and the very first day I observed a woman who was extremely aggressive, manipulative, and carrying a chip on her shoulder. She was so bitter and angry it came through in everything she said. As the facilitator, I commented on this to the people who arranged the session, and they said they were glad I had recognized a behavioral style that was creating problems for the woman. I worked with her to help her see that the upset she's carrying around is creating a self-fulfilling prophecy—and to look at her role in generating the angst.
>
> If a woman is on the receiving end of such negative behaviors, I check how often she has addressed her concern to the

person who is causing the behavior. Many women lack the courage to communicate assertively. To do so, you need to:

- Assume an assertive posture.
- Take a deep breath.
- Use first-person language.
- Develop statements you can use, then practice them.
- Recognize *False Evidence Appearing Real* = FEAR.

Accept that whatever has happened in the past is gone, so if you want a different reality you need to be honest. What's the worst that can happen? Usually, it's that your actions won't be well received, but if you stay stuck in the place of untruth, you will stay there for the rest of your life, and nothing will change for the better.

Most important is looking at what role you have played in creating the scenario. Typically, the world is a mirror.

In her work helping women to change, Race uses the four-phase model of competence that she developed from work by the psychotherapist Carl Rogers.

1. *Unconscious incompetence.* We don't know what we don't know. Our blind spots cover us until we get some feedback, observe, or someone tells us, then we get the awareness to grow.

2. *Conscious incompetence.* We become aware of what we don't know.

3. *Conscious competence.* We make change happen by practicing and trying out new behaviors because we have the information we need. We make conscious choices to gather information and apply it. We develop skill, and after enough practice, it becomes second nature.

4. *Unconscious competence.* At this point, our behavior is automatic.

Race makes the point that we all know how to walk now, but when we were little, we had to learn through trial and error. Changing behavior follows a similar process. She states:

It works. When we take the approach of being mindful of whom we're dealing with and how we want to come across, we're more effective. Bullies come from a place of low self-esteem, little confidence, and intense fear. The only way they know to make themselves feel better is to hurt others. When a bully chooses to look at herself and give herself credit for all the things she has done well and her strengths and abilities, she will stop looking to the outside world for acknowledgment and recognition.

Having applied these principles to her own life, Race can attest to the possibility of transformation. She explains, "I'm a member of a couple of different groups, and there are women who have personality conflicts that incite my negative side. Now I automatically recognize it and say to myself, 'Let me accept her for who she is.'"

Pounds of Prevention

As you read the stories in this book and talk to other women, benefit from the advice they share by using it to shape your own action plan. Determine what tolerable behavior is for you and what is not. Learn more about conflict resolution skills, so you can put these principles to practice in your everyday life.

Merely recognizing behaviors is not enough, though. It will take plenty of practice before your anti-RA way of interacting becomes an ingrained behavior. You can increase the likelihood of this happening by rehearsing new behaviors before you have to use them. The following are some low-level techniques you can try out to get started:

- Practice saying no to a pushy friend who manipulates you to get what she wants. Use the assertive technique of the "broken record," which involves calmly repeating the word no over and over again until the other person gets your message.

- Rehearse assertive behaviors you will use with an aggressive coworker *before* she tries to intimidate and humiliate you. Draw on conflict resolution skills to identify what her motivation is for taking advantage of you, and defuse her abuse. For example, if she repeatedly borrows money from you and doesn't repay it, ask her, as soon as you're seated in the restaurant, if you can borrow money from her because you're short.

- If you're the overly aggressive type, begin to watch yourself in home videos (you might purposely encourage someone in your life to tape frequently). When your guard is down, notice if you tend to dominate conversations and force others to bend to your will. Then practice being silent. See if you can allow a conversation to go on around you without participating beyond a "yes," "I understand," or other brief statements that keep you involved but not intimidating. Transfer that skill to your workplace and situations where you fear you may be the bully.

A Positive You

Another aspect of transforming yourself away from RA is to look at times when you've been helpful to other women, even if you have to stretch a bit to find those situations (family members count). When was the last time another woman thanked you for something you did? What was it that she found particularly beneficial, and can you replicate that behavior again? Are there times you can think of when you helped another woman achieve a goal or worked collaboratively to finish a project? Break down the experience bit by bit and see what your role was, then replicate it. Create your own success again and again, and focus on how you can help the women around you benefit from their interactions with you.

First Impressions Count

Within seconds of meeting another woman, you have formed an impression of her relational style: whether she is open or closed to other women, receptive to the ideas of other women, or fearful of other women. Powerful women take advantage of the opportunity to control their initial interactions with others. The following are some tips to help you think about the image you project, and whether you encourage or discourage other women from pursuing interactions with you:

- Check out a photograph of yourself or look in the mirror without posing. The lines on your face are a giveaway to the expression you habitually project. Are there deep furrows on your forehead from frowning other women away? Do squint lines at the corners of your eyes suggest you may narrow your eyes suspiciously at those you interact with?

- Watch a video where your body language is unguarded. If you want to signal an open, accepting attitude toward others, beware of body language that might contradict this. Your body and brain should convey the same message.

- Review how you establish contacts with other women. Are you the first to say hello? Do you shake hands? Smile?

- Practice introducing yourself to another woman, or interacting with a woman you have RA issues with. Watch your face in the mirror and then listen to your tone of voice to gain clues about the image you project.

- Make a habit of establishing eye contact with other women. Don't stare or invade their body territory, but make a point of connecting visually and smiling.

- Anticipate ahead of time what you want from an encounter with other women. If you're meeting for the first time, are you searching for friends or colleagues? If this is a woman you have a long history of aggression with, are you now hoping to extend the olive branch of forgiveness?

- Prepare a standard set of questions that can be used to draw out other women. Think of things you might have in common with them, and avoid making judgments.

- Compliment a woman to others. If you're with someone else, whether male or female, make a point of commenting on another woman's strengths, whether they be great hostessing style, calm mothering habits, or superior strategic insights at work. Dispel the notion that woman are adversaries, one woman at a time.

- If there is a conflict, ask yourself what you want to happen, and what can help you achieve that result. It takes only a few seconds to figure out if you want to walk away, work the issue out, or put it on the backburner for the time being.

- Be clear on your goals and understand how other women can help you achieve them, and vice versa. Make relationships a win-win situation for both of you.

Learn to Bring Out the Best in Others

Luanne Thorndyke, a physician and the only female associate dean at a large medical school, uses a variety of strategies to promote women. Often, she identifies and advocates for women who may not have received public recognition. It is her policy to publicly make positive statements about these women and to find ways to support them professionally. She believes that little changes for women result in a bigger system change. Thorndyke cites Debra Myerson's book, *Tempered Radicals: How Everyday Leaders Inspire Changes at Work*, as her inspiration and says for her, relationship styles are a value, and the women you affiliate with and how you treat them is part of a value set.

Kare Anderson, a behavioral expert and Emmy-winning former *Wall Street Journal* reporter, discusses how to build personal power while bringing out the best in others. She says that the people who bother you most have the greatest potential to teach you, because learning to deal with their behavior will offer you a "mini–boot camp for dealing with difficult people." Anderson suggests that you can even convert a foe to a friend by figuring out the following:

- What makes her respond positively and negatively to others?
- To what does she devote most of her energy?
- How can you help her change her behavior without making her appear to be wrong?

She also provides a number of strategies for connecting positively with other women, including:

- Make them look good.
- Volunteer something without being asked.
- Make a positive first impression.
- Create a comfortable context for change.
- Draw others out by asking for their opinions and thoughts.

Adopt a Life-Coaching Philosophy

Women rely on one another for intimacy and friendship, but many practice what Phyllis Chesler, author of *Woman's Inhumanity to Woman*, calls sexism toward one another. A new breed of women is looking to change that, by developing strategies for connection that build others up rather than break them down.

As a young girl, if you were involved in a sport or activity, think back on the role your coach or director played. He or she taught you new skills, helped you refine existing ones, and identified areas of strength and ability. When you were discouraged, the coach would cheer you on and inspire you to persevere. He or she was on your side at all times, pushing you to your best performance and providing the support to help you accomplish it.

These are the very skills women excel at and the foundation of a powerful network that can empower you and others. Life coaches are a formal adult version of the schoolteacher who cheered us through adolescence. They are a valuable resource for women who need encouragement and support. Listings of certified coaches can be found in the telephone book and on the Internet, but word of mouth is generally the best way to locate an experienced woman who can meet your needs.

Peace in Our Time

What are the benefits of creating a new relational you? For women who have never had positive relationships with their peers or for those who live lives of fear over possible victimization, freedom from such destructive patterns is an incredible experience. "I never realized how much fun it could be to have women friends," said a reformed bully. "Now I don't have to dread going to work each day," confided a woman who stepped out of the victim role. Middle Bees who gave up gossip and subterfuge found they liked themselves much better once they stopped obsessing over ways to continue as a go-between.

Becoming comfortable with yourself and your interactions with others brings peace to your day-to-day life and opens doors to new opportunities. You can use the skills described in this chapter to change your relationships for the better: start with your friends, then expand to relatives, colleagues, and the community. Savor supportive connections with other women that make each day a blessing rather than a burden.

CHAPTER 17

Don't Stop with Yourself

*Who knows what women can be when they
are finally free to become themselves?*

—BETTY FRIEDAN

Now that you understand and can recognize RA for what it is and have learned to connect with women in more positive and productive ways, take the message beyond your small circle. You may want to start a discussion group, a book club, or a speakers' series. Or, as the women in this chapter did, you may choose to write about these issues for a larger audience.

Continue the Dialogue

Consider the following excerpt titled "Soul Food" by Carolyn Leighton-Tal from the professional organization Women in Technology International (www.witi.com).

> I have always loved thinking deeply about things that intrigue me—I often work puzzles in my head, some of them for years at a time. Although I think of so many different things, my overriding passion since I was a very young girl has been to gain a deep psychological understanding of people and groups.
>
> I am currently working on a puzzle and would appreciate your feedback, since it's so important to consider every possible facet.
>
> I had an interesting conversation several days ago with a

woman working closely with a high-profile executive woman in technology. She confided to me how painful it has been to see this accomplished woman continuously attacked by other women (often in the press)—in proportion, it seemed, to her meteoric rise.

She felt that these women were jealous because the person they were attacking was beautiful and smart and had become very wealthy. She added that she thought this kind of jealousy was a natural feeling among women. My response was that I believed jealously to be more of a reflection of unresolved conflicts from our childhoods.

As I thought about this discussion, I realized this is a topic I want to delve into, since it is an issue that has been raised since WITI started ten years ago. It is also mentioned repeatedly by women attending WITI events.

There seems to be a split among the women I meet—those who operate on the belief system that they will have more if others have less; and those of us who believe we will all have more if we contribute to others having more.

One of my favorite coaches taught me that the first step toward changing behavior requires shifting the belief system upon which this behavior is based. So try giving more instead of less for the next thirty days to those you tend to not support—find out for yourself if "the more you give, the more you get" really works. I personally believe it's much tougher to succeed without the support of others; that you cannot win that support unless you give it. Anyway, it is so much more satisfying knowing you have directly contributed in positive ways to other people's lives.

I like to live by the words of one of my favorite WITI women, Anne Gingras Silver, who told me the first time I met her several years ago, "When I meet people, I focus on our similarities, not our differences."

Relational Monitor

In your new non–RA mode, continue to keep track of your behavior and check out the RA tendencies of those around you. (This will probably come fairly naturally, because once you're sensitized to these dynamics, you quickly see how rampant they are in every-day behavior.) In work, home, and community situations, take the opportunity to help the women around you shift out of aggressive behaviors such as gossip, undermining, and competition. When one woman criticizes another for her faithful adherence to a healthy exercise plan, pipe up and salute her for it. Be the first to recognize and compliment the achievements of both friends and colleagues. Defuse attempts to belittle or humiliate other women by offering supportive comments of your own, and throw in a bit of humor or drama to curtail gossip.

Sometimes bringing in a neutral third party can be a good way to get feedback on your behavior, as well as situations that have you stumped. An older sister who lives a distance away, a mature coworker, someone from your religious organization, or an online pal can all be sources of objective feedback because they don't have the emotional involvement in the immediate situation that you do. They can offer levelheaded advice that may also prompt them to think about how they interact with others.

Keeping a journal or practicing daily meditation focused on opportunities to connect positively with others that you may have previously taken advantage of or failed to appreciate can also help keep you mindful of desired behaviors. It takes only a few minutes to look back over the events of the previous twenty-four hours and reflect on how you related with other women at home, work, or elsewhere.

Mentor Yourself and Others

Given the right motivation and direction, any woman can become a mentor. I've been continually surprised by the ability of high school juniors and seniors to guide younger girls, and the interest of those girls to reach out to their elementary school peers. Sometimes a girl who may not seem a strong candidate as a mentor grows into the role in ways that astonish and touch me deeply. In an article for *Prevention Researcher*, Jennelle Martin, a mentor who worked with me for two years, wrote that her experience with Club Ophelia has given her a lifelong commitment to being a role model and guide for other girls.

Some experts believe women have an inborn advantage when it comes to this role, because our ability to connect socially helps us establish relationships and understand behavior. These qualities make women naturals to motivate, encourage, and support one another.

Mentoring is a deliberate relationship. It's designed to help a protégé learn to use a particular set of skills that can lead to personal and professional advancement. Of course, when your mentor thrives and succeeds, it reflects well on you, too.

As an RA "expert," you can help other women learn to achieve goals without relying on aggression and be a leader in creating and nurturing networks of women. As a mentor, your role modeling, facilitation, networking, advice, and leadership can help overcome RA in the workplace, community organization, volunteer group, or other endeavor you share. To learn more or explore how you can become your own mentor, see appendix D.

Become a Networking Queen

To network is to build up a system of contacts and supports that will help you achieve your goal or mutual goals. In her article "Why Networking Clubs Aren't Just for the Boys," *Wall Street Journal* reporter Susan Wilson Solovic encourages women to join specialty organizations relevant to their interests, then draw on personal resources such as friends, family, and acquaintances as a way of building their own network. Since the human component of connecting with others is essential to effective networking, women have an innate ability to excel at this. Solovic reminds us to begin by extending help to others before expecting them to do things for us, and to allow ourselves plenty of time to build a rich network to which we never stop adding.

As a woman concerned about RA, building a network of like-minded colleagues can help you continue to spread the word and meet others who share your vision of helping women to forge healthier relationships with one another. All of your networking colleagues can then go on to build further resources of their own that will benefit them, you, and other women.

What About Men?

Although men don't gravitate toward RA in the same way women do, there certainly are men who use this behavior or, at a minimum, reinforce it in women. As you change the way you relate to women, you also are likely to change the way you relate to men and your willingness to accept the mean girl stereotype. This effect can be contagious, so that Queen Bees and Middle Bees find their aggression thwarted, as happened in one large medical practice. A particularly vicious Queen Bee was told by her male boss to change her behavior or leave, after receiving complaints from employees of both genders about the woman's hostile treatment of other women.

Counteract Negative Media Messages

Despite the evidence that a serious problem exists in women's relationships, there is still denial and reluctance to take action to address it. Judith Briles, a true expert on workplace relationships and the author of several books on women's relationships (*Woman to Woman 2000: Becoming Sabotage Savvy and Woman to Woman: From Sabotage to Support*), has completed extensive studies and offered countless workshops on bullying. She continues to meet resistance from some media sources, who seem to want to perpetuate the image of desperate and aggressive women. For example, when articles describing RA between female health-care workers appeared in two magazines with national distribution, Briles promptly contacted the editors and offered to share her expertise to educate and inform readers about RA. In both situations, not only was her offer rejected, but her communications to the editors were never published. Fortunately, this hasn't deterred pioneer Briles from continuing to educate and change the attitudes of both women and men. Demian Yumei, an Internet pal, e-mailed me the following not long ago:

> I submitted a proposal to iVillage.com to host a board on relational aggression, and I was very clear on my purpose and how I wanted to handle the situation. I invited them to look at my Web site, see what I was about as a singer/songwriter and human-rights activist, as well as read the short essay I wrote on

relational aggression. They wrote back and said "Thank you but no thank you." They did not feel the topic was appropriate for iVillage! I know iVillage is about empowering women, and I understand that many women's-rights activists are afraid to look at this "dark side" of femininity for fear of the catty stereotype. But I think it's the very refusal to see this side of ourselves that lends to this mean-spirited type of covert aggression that relational aggression is all about.

There is another board that does cover relational aggression quite a bit, but they don't call it that. The board is titled "Toxic Relationships" (http://messageboards.ivillage.com/iv-rltoxicrelat), but it's amazing how many posts are just about relationship aggression, backstabbing among women. I guess you can talk about it as long as you don't call it by its name and acknowledge its pervasiveness among women. Funny, huh? I guess the term *toxic relationships* is safe because it's inclusive, and we don't have to acknowledge its specificity as a means of aggression among women. What are we so afraid about?

The message board at the site Demian referred to is indeed rife with posts about relationships between women in which aggression is the destructive dynamic. Enjoy2003 wrote about breaking off a relationship with a friend who was overly aggressive. Mizdiana described grief over being deliberately excluded by a woman she considered a friend, calling it one of the most painful experiences of her adult life.

As part of reaching out to others, you can set up and host your own message board, where alternative approaches to RA are discussed and disseminated or you're welcome to use my Web site, www.cheryldellasega.com, for that purpose. The site will provide an opportunity for women to have discussions on both problems and opportunities.

Another woman, who prefers to remain anonymous, contacted me with the following story of a major cover-up of RA by the media.

Speak Truth to Power, with Power

This is an insider's account regarding a young woman who was subjected to violence gone wild in the workplace. In 1998, while working as an executive assistant to an international celebrity, the young woman was terrorized and even assaulted several times. When asked why she took the job, the victim said, "I saw a recent program where [the bully] teamed with Nelson Mandela to help children and thought I'd be able to be part of a group that could make great things happen globally."

The victim did not engage in the tabloid exploitation of her harassment and assault in order to assure and to uphold her credibility, but she was hounded by the press and treated as if she were at fault. Her voice was unheard, and she spent painful, lonely hours dealing with PTSD (posttraumatic stress disorder), physical and emotional repercussions, an unbearable justice system, and a manipulated media's wrongful calculated reporting.

In an effort for the truth to be heard, friends appealed to the editor at *Vogue* magazine. The powers that be at *Vogue* responded with a full five-page spread glamorizing the bully celebrity. The celebrity was praised on her wardrobe and mug shot at the fingerprinting. The media and highly skilled public-relations strategies made sure that every twist was turned in favor of the celebrity involved.

There was never an apology from the publication to the victim once the guilty verdict rang out from both criminal and civil courts. Gag laws wouldn't allow the true story to be told by the victim, but they didn't stop the bully from appearing on national television and reinforcing her lies about the incident to preserve her reputation.

The victim (she cringes when she hears this title, because in all that she endured she tried not to take that stance) had also appealed to Dr. Phil for guidance. After several attempts to get his response, he told her she needed a $25,000 retainer or he would not even look at her case. He mentioned proudly on a telecall that his clients were high-profile individuals, newscasters, and celebrities.

My friend, a highly competent, caring, spiritual individual, has lost friends and jobs, suffered financial and health issues, and did not deserve one moment of this. She has decided to immerse herself in compassionate world causes and volunteers her services endlessly, hoping in time that her stress-induced ailments will become less consuming by promoting noble acts and peace.

Perhaps you can be the one to help "speak truth to power."

We cannot allow media delusions to rule, or mass support of such behaviors, especially upholding two-faced celebrity bullies in the name of beauty, rank, and power.

Exposing incidents of RA and being supportive of women who may have been overpowered by someone with more money or status is an outreach effort every woman can make. Even adolescent girls share situations where they have taken a chance and spoken truth to power, as this author describes.

Raise Awareness

Be verbal and visible about your commitment to change, so that it makes you more accountable to others. Talk to other women one-on-one, write reviews about books that celebrate female connections, and don't hesitate to point out RA-type behaviors when you see them. (My Club and Camp Ophelia participants have taught me to do with honor and grace.) Lobby against images or activities that promote hostile competition between women, such as slanted newspaper articles, television shows that pit one woman against another to win the favors of a man, and advertisements that portray two women vying with each other for the attention of a man. In the same way, applaud efforts to celebrate women's connections, and consider ways that you and other women can contribute to changing the public perception of women. This could be through creativity (writing, art, or another form of expression) or by forming a support or discussion group for the purpose of developing a plan of action.

The concept of "friendship circles" where women can explore connections with one another and discover their spirituality is further evidence that others believe woman-to-woman support is important. In her book *The Millionth Circle*, Jean Shinodan Bolan suggests that if enough women adopt new patterns of behavior based on nurturing and helping each other, we can eventually alter the psyche of the human race.

Keep learning and empowering yourself and others. At every opportunity unite with other women to promote positive opportunities for all women. The richer your network of connections with women (that is, trustworthy women whom you've helped in one way or another) the more successful you personally will become.

Love or Leave the Bees

There will still be Queen Bee women in your life whom you're forced to associate with, even if you change jobs, resign from a community organization, or quit your gym. You and the women around you who understand the dynamics of RA can reach out to these women with compassion, and try to help them change for the better, which, given the strong personalities of many Queen Bees, would be a great contribution. Imagine the potential of all the Queen Bees and Middle Bees devoting themselves to support rather than sabotage.

When reform isn't possible, the best strategy may be to limit your contact with such women, knowing they will drain you of energy and enthusiasm. One of my closest colleagues and I recently encountered a situation that put us both on "sabotage alert." After trying for months to forge a more fulfilling and positive interaction with the Queen Bee network, we decided to honor our commitments and then move on, continuing with our own collaboration. It was a matter of using our time effectively: why struggle to accomplish smaller transactions with the other group when during an equal amount of time we could easily work with each other to accomplish mutual far-reaching goals?

Organizations to Help

There are organizations you can turn to for help, support, and guidance, whether you seek to change your life professionally or personally. Consider Sonya, who joined a group of women training for a triathlon and learned to step out of the victim role she had long occupied at work. Darcy, a former Middle Bee fond of gossip, discovered her energies could be spent more productively in Zonta, a women's service organization. Traci, an entrenched Queen Bee in her local PTA, became part of a writers group and discovered that expressing her feelings in written words rather than aggressive behaviors not only put her in touch with a creativity she didn't know she possessed, but improved her relationships with other mothers.

Create a Better Place for Girls

Just as older women can learn how to develop positive peer relationships, young women in the next generation can learn skills that will put them in good stead throughout adulthood. Act as a role model so your daughter and other young women learn attitudes of cooperation from you, rather than competition. Teach them to express their emotions in ways that aren't hurtful to another woman, and discuss the importance of and differences between relationships and friendships. Use daily events at home, work, and school to explore ways to avoid victimization or aggression.

Understanding RA will help younger women deal with painful incidents, both past and present. As one young woman who worked on several projects related to RA told me, "I wish I had known this when I was in school, but now I'm going to do everything possible to help younger women deal with these issues."

Relational Appreciation

While women are quick to recognize the shortcomings of one another, and, if inclined to RA, express those perceptions hurtfully, the flip side of relationships isn't always true. Change these tendencies by making it a habit to thank the women who enrich your life in various ways. A telephone call to say, "I really appreciated you helping me with that fund-raiser," or an e-mail that shares "It's so much easier to train for a triathlon with you by my side. Thanks!" can be brief but effective ways of recognizing the support of other women. In the work setting, express gratitude toward women who have supported you, whether your career is in or outside the home, or both. Hearing that they have made a positive difference can be empowering for women who are part of our everyday lives but often overlooked.

In the same way, RA-free relationships with women need to be cherished and cared for. Just as you would preserve a car, a favorite blouse, or a piece of jewelry, so, too, should you tend to your friendships. Tell trusted friends and loyal colleagues regularly how much they mean to you, and make sure they gain as much from the relationship as you do.

In her article "The Healing Power of Friendship," journalist Melinda Marshall, a contributor to *Ladies Home Journal*, suggests the following strategies to nurture your gal pals:

- Rather than waiting for invitations, invite others or stage an event of your own.

- Talk about your insecurities and fears. Marshall says, "A good way to bypass all that nasty one-upmanship women engage in when they feel insecure is simply to throw your insecurity on the table."

- Get to know the friends of your friends, creating what Marshall calls an instant network. These are women you already share something with—a gal pal.

- Invest time and energy in developing and maintaining relationships.

In the same way, you can show your colleagues at work and volunteer, sports, or other organizations how much you appreciate them by:

- Voicing thanks—both after specific projects and activities and in general.

- Inviting them to be part of committees, groups, or other endeavors that you are in charge of, specifically noting how positive your previous collaborations have been.

- Giving them sincere compliments in the presence of others: "Donna is a whiz at grant writing" or "Linda is a great committee chair."

- Asking for their assistance, advice, or opinion because you respect their talents and wisdom.

- Introducing them to each other, so more women can benefit from their expertise and ability.

- Sending them copies of articles or other information you think they might find interesting or helpful.

From This Point On

Four years ago, I began writing about mothering my teen daughter and the challenges we confronted. Through connections with other women, that writing became a book that touched many lives. My second book examined another painful issue: aggression in adolescent girls. As I gathered material from a variety of sources, I connected with women in places as far away as Alaska and New Zealand and as close as the town next to mine. A third book on the response of mothers to children with eating disorders again reminded me of the incredible power women have to support one another through good and bad times.

This book has given me another opportunity to hear from and collaborate with like-minded women who believe in the positive potential of female relationships. Again, the real-time and virtual bonding has been surprising, enlightening, and uplifting.

The Beat Goes On

Around the time I began writing this book, I had lunch with Carol, a nurse practitioner colleague, and friend who was caught in the middle of a classic Queen Bee work situation. Never a gossip, Carol spent most of our time together during that lunch wondering how she would survive her hostile work environment, despite the strong commitment she felt to her patients. Soon after, Carol resigned her position, much to the regret of most of her coworkers. (The Queen Bee and her minions remained in place and didn't bother to attend her going-away party.)

If the encounter with Carol convinced me that there needs to be a national awareness of adult RA, another lunch renewed my belief in the ability of women to support one another to end this dynamic. In June 2003, I sat at a table in a restaurant with three women who had mysteriously come into my life at opportune moments. To my right was Jessica, a college student, who had e-mailed me out of the blue, asking if I might hire her to help with my summer programs for girls. I had misguidedly believed I could somehow do all the work by myself, but when this bright young woman came to my office for an interview, I knew she was the person who could help me be more organized and productive.

Two other women shared our lunch. Olivia, an Asian American graduate student was there because she wanted to help with my Club Ophelia Web site. Her commitment to overcoming RA came from personal experiences and a desire to make things better for other girls.

Suzanne, another engaging graduate student, had recently returned to school after a career in public relations. Her interest in the well-being of girls had been sparked by her mother, a colleague of mine who also offers programs on RA.

None of us knew one another well, but as we discussed the collaboration we were about to undertake for the summer, our mutual interests sparked a lively and synergistic conversation. Listening to the insights and wisdom of each young woman, I was struck by my good fortune in being part of such a team.

I happened to describe that meeting to a colleague a short time later.

"How do you find such interesting people?" she asked. "There's always someone new and fascinating that you just 'happen to meet.'"

I hadn't thought about it before, but she was right. An incredible number of gifted women have come my way, some to help me achieve goals, others to offer support, and the rest to just "be." How rewarding it is to connect with individuals or groups who can enrich our lives, and, hopefully, be equally grateful for their encounters with us.

Long ago, my mother was a role model who revealed the rewards of female friendships to me. As an adult, my life has been like hers—filled with diverse women who enrich the day-to-day activities of work, home, and play. I hope I'll continue to enjoy female friends and colleagues into old age, just as she has.

For everyone out there who has grown up without these kinds of relationships, you will be surprised to discover what you've missed for so many years. Step away from the mean stereotypes we as women have dragged around since girlhood, and take a new look at your peers. In every area of life, there are many who can bring the special gifts of sisterhood: understanding, support, insight, caring, and much more. How can you deny yourself—or the women around you—such a gift?

Communication That Counts

Connecting through Words

There are many aspects of communication that can help or hinder a relationship. Consider the following tips as part of your strategy for avoiding relationally aggressive interactions.

Nonverbals

Effectively communicating with others involves more than choosing the right words. Consider each of the following behaviors as part of sending an effective message.

- Posture. How you stand, sit, and walk projects a message about how you feel about yourself. A woman who shuffles into a room with her shoulders slumped makes a dramatically different impression than one who walks in with her back straight and head level.

- Facial expressions. The face is often a direct mirror of the emotions. All too often frowning, staring, or sighing can be habits that convey a negative message when none is intended.

- Gestures. Any movements you make with your hands or other part of your body can contradict or overemphasize the content of your words. Toe tapping, leg bouncing, crossed arms, and other unconscious gestures may suggest to others that you are uncomfortable, bored, or intimidated by them, even when this isn't the case.

- Clothing and appearance. Especially for women, what you wear and how you appear are often interpreted as signs of who you are and how you feel about others. Compare the mental image and associated feelings you have about a woman in a business suit, stockings, and high heels versus a woman in khakis and a plain shirt.

- Eye contact. The trick here is to gauge how comfortable others are with eye contact, and adjust your behavior accordingly. Eye contact that is too intense may be perceived of as aggressive while avoiding eye contact may be regarded as passive.

- Personal space. Some women feel threatened if you stand too close when you're talking to them, while others are offended by too much distance. If someone shifts away or shrinks from you physically, take the hint that they feel you're intruding on their space. Hugging is always a tricky practice that is more common among women than men. Before you hug someone, be aware of other cues about personal space that will let you know if the gesture is welcome.

Using Words Assertively

Getting your message across in a nonhurtful way involves both your tone of voice and the words you choose. Confusing aggressiveness with assertiveness is a common mistake, but there's a clear difference. Assertive communication is win-win communication that doesn't hurt you or the person you're talking to. Aggression does. Some techniques to help you assert yourself include:

- Beginning the conversation with a neutral topic.

- Expressing your intent to discuss the issue at hand, whether it's the need for a favor or a dispute that needs resolved. For example, say, "I'd like to talk about what happened at the soccer game yesterday."

- Using "I" statements to show that you are speaking only for yourself. Instead of saying "You should lower your voice," substitute "I wish you would lower your voice when we're together." "You always make fun of me in front of others" becomes "It bothers me when you make fun of me in front of others."

- Owning your feelings. Admit that your feelings may not be shared by others.

- Tell what would be helpful to you in the situation, but phrase it as a request. An example would be: "From now on when we go shopping together could you try not to criticize my parenting style?"

- Admit culpability. Don't be afraid to say you're sorry when you've done something wrong, or admit when you've made a mistake.

- Express appreciation. "Thanks for taking the time to talk about this."

Encouraging Dialogue Instead of Directives

The best communication is mutual. Rather than aggressively monopolizing a conversation, use these strategies to interact with others in ways that foster rather than fray interactions:

- Make requests. Instead of demanding or ordering, ask. Even if you are the boss, a request is always received better than an imperative. "Could you get this done by three?" is likely to garner better results than "Do this by three."

- Ask for clarification. If you aren't sure you've been understood, get more information in a nonthreatening way. For example, try "Could you say more about that?" "I'm not sure I understood the part about . . . ," or "So if I'm following you correctly, you want . . . "

- Be honest. Admit if you don't know something, and ask for help finding out, if appropriate. If you're not sure you're right, don't pass information on until you've verified it. "I'll get back to you on that" or "I'll have an answer for you in five minutes" are positive ways of responding when you're not sure of the correct answer.

- Use silence. Allow for pauses in the conversation, or deliberately reflect on what's been said. Don't jump in to speak the moment there's silence.

- Listen as much as you talk. The woman who speaks nonstop

without picking up on the cues of her listeners is communicating aggressively. To avoid dominating the conversation, try to track how much you are talking and give others an equal opportunity.

- Keep the conversation going with open-ended questions. To get the most information and understanding, ask questions that can't be answered with a simple yes or no. Beginning with words like "How did," "What do," or "Describe for me" will help enrich another person's answers and elaborate on their thoughts.

- Nod your head. Give a "go on" signal by nodding your head or otherwise encouraging the speaker. "Hmm" or "Say more" will help others feel comfortable sharing with you.

Your Delivery

If you are about to engage in a conversation that has the potential to cause conflict, consider these tips:

- Don't let emotion overwhelm you. If you are angry, cool off before speaking with others.

- Make sure you speak clearly. Don't mumble or hesitate because it makes you sound indecisive. Speak loud enough to be heard, but don't raise your voice. Avoid putting your hands or anything else in front of your mouth that might block the words.

- Don't interrupt. Make sure the other person is finished speaking before you jump in.

- Be consistent. Don't overwhelm someone with conversation one day and ignore her the next.

- Be prepared. Practice what you want to say ahead of time, regardless of whether you anticipate difficulty or not.

- Keep the initial conversation simple. Try to talk through one specific issue before you tackle a lifetime of problems you want to work through with the other person.

Talking to Yourself in Ways That Help

Even the best intentions to overcome RA and communicate effectively can be derailed by negative self-talk. Afraid-to-Bees in particular can be at risk for staying silent due to internal messages that negate the value of their opinions and feelings, but women in other "Bee" roles can also be struggling with inner voices that lead to aggressive and hurtful responses to others. Because most of our emotions come from the mental messages we give ourselves every day, an important aspect of overcoming RA is to explore this process further.

Take some time to listen to messages you give yourself that may either encourage or discourage a sense of self-worth, thereby fueling any one of the RA roles described in this book. Following are some steps that can help with this process, used with permission from the Web site "Manage Your Self Talk" (www.pe2000.com/anx-selftalk.htm). The site is part of the Pegasus NLP Mind-Body Health Site and is maintained by Reg Connolly, Psychotherapist and NLP Practitioner.

Pay Attention to Your Negative Self-Hypnosis

Begin to pay attention to your self-talk. That's the constant stream of chatter that goes on in your head (and mine, and everyone else's, by the way).

Notice what you say to yourself and how you say it. Do you constantly criticize yourself inside your head? Or do you constantly criticize others? Or complain about your life, your faults, or how life "treats" you? Or internally rant about the injustices of life?

Do you constantly tell yourself you're at your wits' end? Or that you can't cope with this much longer? Or that you'll fail at something? Or that you're going to have a panic attack?

Imagine that you had an "invisible friend" that went around with you all day, every day, and was constantly whispering comments like these in your ear. How would you feel at the end of a day? At the end of a week? A month?

Well, guess what? You're already doing this to yourself—and in a far more effective manner that this invisible friend would do it, because you could reject what the friend says or politely tell her to go elsewhere with her comments.

Negative self-talk is pernicious, demoralizing, and debilitating. And you get so used to doing it and responding to it that you don't consciously pay attention to it. You are, in effect, continuously giving yourself very powerful hypnotic suggestions to feel bad!

Gently Replace the Negative Self-Talk

I say gently, because there's no point in adding to the inner stress by arguing with yourself by saying "I must not say this" etc.

Each time you recognize the inner-undermining going on, pause; remind yourself that it's just the old habit you got into, and that you're now changing this habit. Use a very soft and patient inner tone of voice for this. You inner voice should sound as if you are calming an upset two-year-old. Reassure yourself. Calm yourself. Remind yourself of the rationales and facts of the situation. Remind yourself of the value of handling things in a cool, calm, and confident manner.

Doing this once or twice won't make a lot of difference. It takes quite a while to replace the habits of a lifetime, but it's definitely worth doing.

APPENDIX C

Netiquette Tips

Tone of voice, facial expressions, and other forms of body language reinforce words and underlying emotions when women communicate. All of these cues are lost in an e-mail, so take extra care when crafting a message in order to avoid inadvertent relational aggression. Try the following:

- Use complete sentences and proper punctuation so your intent is clear. For example, write "I would appreciate it if we could get together to talk about something that happened between us in high school" instead of "We need to talk. I know it was a long time ago but it's important."

- Never use all caps, and be sparing with exclamation points. Write "Let me know what you think about my suggestion," instead of: "LET ME KNOW WHAT YOU THINK!!!!"

- Don't rely on hidden meanings; spell out your feelings and thoughts. Write "I feel sort of awkward even bringing up the past, but it's important to me" instead of "We need to talk about this."

- Ask for confirmation that your message has been received. If you don't hear back, it doesn't necessarily mean she's ignoring you; she may not check her e-mail frequently, or her system may be down.

- Don't send repeated e-mails if she chooses not to respond to you.

- Don't use profanity or threats in your e-mail.

- Consider having a friend read the e-mail before you send it, or save it on your computer and reread it another day before sending it.

- Sign your e-mail with your real name and, in parentheses, the name you used when she knew you.

- Make your first e-mail brief and to the point. If you both choose to continue corresponding by e-mail, print out a copy of each message. Read a hard copy of her messages before responding to them.

- Don't respond immediately to her e-mails. Give yourself an hour or a day to think over what you want to say, because quick emotional e-mails may not communicate in a positive way.

Mentoring Resources

Do you want to gain inspiration from other women who serve as role models for positive relationship skills? Read the following books alone or in a group, and identify the strategies used to forge "powHERful" female connections.

Mentoring Heroes: 52 Fabulous Women's Paths to Success and the Mentors Who Empowered Them, by author Mary K. Doyle. Doyle describes how both high-profile and ordinary women benefited from mentoring relationships. Those profiled include the actress and motivational speaker Ann Jillian, several high-powered female executives, a judge, and ordinary women such as a Catholic nun, a rabbi, a stockbroker, a lawyer, a dentist, a hairdresser, a psychologist, a probation officer, and a nurse. The title was derived from the conclusion that the right mentor can make a critical difference in the life of a woman.

Women Who Could . . . And Did: Lives of 26 Exemplary Artists and Scientists by Karma Kitaj, Ph.D. Dr. Kitaj is an experienced psychotherapist who began this work as a study of career success in several prominent artists and scientists. As she wrote about these women, Dr. Kitaj realized that the stories of their lives were so inspiring they could help readers who faced similar challenges. Three winning behaviors that many of these women used were passion, perseverance, and power with others. Strategies that helped them overcome failures included energy, focus, obstinacy, being able to let go, trusting themselves, enjoying hard work, a sense of self competence, and taking risks. The book is described as a paper mentor for women who lack access to true mentors.

Be Your Own Mentor: Strategies from Top Women on the Secrets of Success by Sheila Wellington of Catalyst, a women's research organization. This book advises women on how to find a mentor as well as the skills needed to become a mentor for yourself and others. This book is loaded with information and encouragement as well as practical advice.

The 12 Secrets of Highly Creative Women: A Portable Mentor by Gail McMeekin. This book contains stories of forty-five women who achieved their dreams. McMeekin hopes the book will be a portable mentor for women who seek to transform their lives. Three principles guide McMeekin's advice: creativity, resource building, and prioritizing.

Learning from Other Women: How to Benefit from the Knowledge, Wisdom, and Experience of Female Mentors, by Carolyn S. Duff. Duff is president of a consulting firm that deals with gender issues and believes women need to use one another (rather than men) as mentors. Using input from two hundred career women, the book contains suggestions on finding the right mentor and fostering mentoring relationships. Duff also added a wealth of resources, including some worksheets and Web sites and other reading materials.

References

Anderson, Kare (2004). *"Everyday Ways to Bring Out Their Best Side and Build Your Positive Influence."* See her Web site at www.sayitbetter.com for other valuable resources.

Ashcroft, Mary Ellen (1991). *Temptations Women Face: Honest Talk about Jealousy, Anger, Sex, Money, Food, Pride.* Downers Grove, IL: InterVarsity Press.

Astin, Helen, and Carole Leland (1991). *Women of Influence, Women of Vision: A Cross-Generational Study of Leaders and Social Change.* San Francisco: Jossey-Bass.

Bolan, Jean Shinodan (1999). *The Millionth Circle: How to Change Ourselves and the World—The Essential Guide to Women's Circles.* York Beach, ME: Conari.

Boothman, Nicholas (2000). *How to Make People Like You in 90 Seconds or Less.* NY: Workman Publishing.

Briles, Judith (1989). *Woman to Woman: From Sabotage to Support.* Far Hills, NJ: New Horizon Press.

——— (1994). *The Briles Report on Women in Healthcare: Changing Conflict to Collaboration in a Toxic Workplace.* San Francisco: Jossey-Bass.

——— (1999). *Woman to Woman 2000: Becoming Sabotage Savvy in the New Millennium.* Far Hills, NJ: New Horizon Press.

Brinkman, Rick, and Rick Kirschner (2002). *Dealing with People You Can't Stand: How to Bring Out the Best in People at Their Worst.* NY: McGraw-Hill.

Campbell, Anne (1993). *Men, Women, and Aggression.* NY: Basic Books.

Chesler, Phyllis (2003). *Woman's Inhumanity to Woman.* NY: Plume Books.

Connolly, Reg (2000). *Manage Your Self-Talk.* www.pe2000.com/neg-hypnosis.htm.

Davis, Laura (2002). *I Thought We'd Never Speak Again: The Road from Estrangement to Reconciliation.* NY: HarperCollins.

Doyle, Mary K. (2000). *Mentoring Heroes: 52 Fabulous Women's Paths to Success and the Mentors Who Empowered Them.* Geneva, IL: 3E Press.

Duff, Carolyn (1999). *Learning from Other Women: How to Benefit from the Knowledge, Wisdom, and Experience of Female Mentors.* NY: AMACOM Press.

Freeman, Sue, Susan Bourque, and Christine Shelton, eds. (2001). *Women on Power: Leadership Redefined*. Boston: Northeastern University Press.

Friday, Nancy (1997). *The Power of Beauty: Men, Women and Sex Appeal Since Feminism*. NY: HarperCollins.

Gilligan, Carol (1993). *In a Different Voice: Psychological Theory and Women's Development*. Boston: Harvard University Press.

Gilligan, Carol, and Lyn Mikel Brown (1993). *Meeting at the Crossroads*. NY: Ballantine Books.

Golden, Marita (October 2002). "White Women at Work," *Essence Magazine*.

Hammers, Maryann (November 2003). "Stand Up for Yourself." *Fitness Magazine*.

Heim, Pat, and Susan Murphy, with Susan Golant (2001). *In the Company of Women: Turning Workplace Conflict into Powerful Alliances*. NY: Penguin-Putnam.

Helgesen, Sally (1995). *The Female Advantage: Women's Ways of Leadership*. NY: Doubleday.

Hibbard, Ann (1999). *Treasured Friends: Finding and Keeping True Friendships*. Grand Rapids, MI: Baker Books.

Hollands, Jean (2002). *Same Game, Different Rules: How to Get Ahead without Being a Bully Boss, Ice Queen, or Ms. Understood*. NY: McGraw-Hill.

Jackson, Linda (1992). *Physical Appearance and Gender: Sociobiological and Sociocultural Perspectives*. Albany, NY: State University of New York Press.

Joyner, Tammy (September 4, 2001). "Bully Bosses Find Their Gentler Side: Makeover Programs Helping Women 'Walk a Finer Line' as Top Managers." *Atlanta Journal and Constitution*.

Kirkpatrick, Kathyrn (Summer 2003). "Her Hatred." *Rattle Magazine*.

Kitaj, Karma (2002). *Women Who Could . . . and Did: Lives of 26 Exemplary Artists and Scientists*. Chestnut Hill, MA: Huckle Hill Press.

Leighton-Tal, Carolyn (2001). "Soul Food." www.witi.org/wire/feature/cleighton/archives/200001/. Also see the Web site www.witi.com.

Lein, Laura, and Marvin Sussman (1983). *The Ties That Bind: Men's and Women's Social Networks*. NY: Haworth Press.

Mallick, Heather (July 28, 1996). "Beautiful Losers." *The Toronto Sun*.

Mandel, Deborah (2003). *Healing the Sensitive Heart: How to Stop Getting Hurt, Build Your Inner Strength, and Find the Love You Deserve*. Avon, MA: Adams Media Corporation. See also her Web site www.sensitive-heart.com.

Martin, Jennelle (2004). "Mentoring." *Prevention Researcher*.

McMeekin, Gail (2000). *The 12 Secrets of Highly Creative Women: A Portable Mentor*. York Beach, ME: Red Wheel/Weiser.

Myerson, Debra (2003). *Tempered Radicals: How Everyday Leaders Inspire Change at Work*. Boston: Harvard University Press.

Nadien, Margot, and Florence Denmark, eds. (1992). *Females and Autonomy: A Lifespan Perspective*. Boston: Allyn and Bacon.

Naistadt, Ivy (2004). *Speak without Fear: A Total System for Becoming a Natural, Confident Communicator.* NY: HarperCollins.

Nicholson, Nigel (June 2001). "Evolved to Chat: The New Word on Gossip," *Psychology Today.*

Race, Susan (1999). *Succeeding in the Workplace: Critical Skills for a Rewarding Career and the Life You Love.* Yardley, PA: Personal Growth Systems. Her Web site is www.personalgrowthsystems.com.

Rourke, Brian (October 5, 2002). "Battling Female Aggression." *The Providence Journal.*

Schwartz, Dianne (2000). *Whose Face Is in the Mirror? The Story of One Woman's Journey from the Nightmare of Domestic Abuse to True Healing.* CA: Hay House.

Sere, A. (1999). "My Passion for Women." www.saidit.org.

Sheehy, Sandy (2000). *Connecting: The Enduring Power of Female Friendship.* NY: William Morrow.

Small, Linda Lee (March 2003). "What White Women Are Really Saying About Us!" *Essence Magazine.*

Solovic, Susan Wilson (November 4, 2003). "Why Networking Clubs Aren't Just for the Boys." The *Wall Street Journal.*

Southam, Kate (June 24, 2003). "Bully Bosses Bad for Your Health." www.shesaid.com.au/article/2003/06/24/1017_wl.htm.

Sutphen, Judith (April 8, 2002). "Mean Girls." www.women.state. vt.us/meangirls.html.

Tanenbaum, Leora (2002). *Catfight: Rivalries among Women—from Diets to Dating, from the Boardroom to the Delivery Room.* NY: HarperCollins.

Taylor, Shelley (2003). *The Tending Instinct: Women, Men, and the Biology of Relationships.* NY: Owl Books.

Underwood, Jim (2003). *More Than a Pink Cadillac: Mary Kay Inc.'s 9 Leadership Keys to Success.* NY: McGraw Hill.

Weikle, Julia. www.indiana.edu/~eric_rec/ieo/digests/d84.html.

Weiner, David (2002). *Power Freaks: Dealing with Them in the Workplace or Anyplace.* NY: Prometheus Books.

Wellington, Sheila (2001). *Be Your Own Mentor: Strategies from Top Women on the Secrets of Success.* NY: Random House.

White, Kate (1996). *Why Good Girls Don't Get Ahead . . . but Gutsy Girls Do: Nine Secrets Every Working Woman Must Know.* NY: Warner Books.

Yager, Jan (1999). *Friendshifts: The Power of Friendship and How It Shapes Our Lives.* Stamford, CT: Hannacroix Creek Books.

——— (2002). *When Friendship Hurts: How to Deal with Friends Who Betray, Abandon, or Wound You.* NY: Fireside.

Index